E-Portfolios for Educational Leaders

An ISLLC-Based Framework for Self-Assessment

Barbara L. Nicholson

ScarecrowEducation
Lanham, Maryland • Toronto • Oxford
2004

Published in the United States of America
by ScarecrowEducation
An imprint of The Rowman & Littlefield Publishing Group, Inc.
4501 Forbes Boulevard, Suite 200, Lanham, Maryland 20706
www.scarecroweducation.com

PO Box 317
Oxford
OX2 9RU, UK

British Library Cataloguing in Publication Information Available

Library of Congress Cataloging-in-Publication Data

Nicholson, Barbara L., 1951–
  E-portfolios for educational leaders : an ISLLC-based framework for self-assessment / Barbara L. Nicholson.
    p. cm.
  Includes bibliographical references and index.
  ISBN 1-57886-092-X (pbk. : alk. paper)
  1. Portfolios in education—Computer-aided design. 2. School administrators—Training of. 3. Educational leadership—Evaluation. I. Title.
LB1029.P67 N53 2004
371.2'011—dc22

2003020558

∞™ The paper used in this publication meets the minimum requirements of American National Standard for Information Sciences—Permanence of Paper for Printed Library Materials, ANSI/NISO Z39.48-1992.
Manufactured in the United States of America.

Contents

Preface

This book grew out of a need to provide preservice principals entering Marshall University's Graduate School of Education and Professional Development a rationale and framework for developing the portfolios they submit as part of the requirement for obtaining their master's degrees in leadership studies. Its primary quality, thus, is functionalist. It is, however, fair to say that the genesis for both the portfolio project and this book was in large part philosophical, grounded in what we, the faculty, think about how students learn and what we think about institutions of higher learning and their relationships with their students and the broader education community.

Our leadership studies faculty share some fundamental principles. Chief among them is a belief that at the heart of every educator's philosophy should lie a commitment to ensuring that each and every student has a chance to succeed. As educators of future school administrators, then, we see our own responsibility as threefold: providing access to the knowledge and skills necessary for students' growth and development; giving them opportunities to actualize their learning in a "real" school environment; and encouraging a disposition for reflective practice.

A reexamination of those principles in light of an extensive program review, however, suggested that we had insufficient evidence to confirm that we were meeting that responsibility. The catalyst for this program conversion, in part, was a deepening dissatisfaction with the comprehensive examination as an instrument for evaluating either potential graduates' proficiencies or our own program. Its deficiencies, as we saw them, were multiple.

Although the centrality of an accepted knowledge base is, as many accrediting agencies believe, a function of the kind of education reform currently sought, neither a standardized licensing test nor a comprehensive examination of students' "knowledge" provided a complete picture of our students' abilities to perform as effective school administrators. Further, occurring as they did at the end of the student's matriculation, they were essentially irremediable. As is related to program evaluation, one could reasonably consider the percentage rate of students passing the comprehensive exam and our state's administrative licensing test (the Praxis II) viable measures of curricular success; and those measures, have, in fact, reflected a level of programmatic success well above average. Still, our interest in outcomes other than cognitive capability rendered those measures problematic.

Test scores do little to reveal whether any of the "knowledge" educators routinely dispense in the classroom is of value to the students. The academic integrity of any given program of study should center on its knowledge utilization (i.e., on the degree to which its graduates find their learning experiences useful in the world of practice). This is especially the case in education where both teacher and administrative preparation programs have been roundly criticized for being out of touch with what actually goes on in schools. Analyzing examination data does nothing to mitigate that criticism, much of which has been shown to be justified.

Compounding those issues was a migration from a traditional campus-based program to a course delivery system that combines occasional on-site meetings with online instruction, making a progressive assessment method that features ongoing interaction between students and faculty even more important. With the reduction in face-to-face contact that characterizes computer-assisted instruction, relying solely on students' grades in discrete courses and the kind of summative evaluation represented by the comprehensive or licensing exams seemed not only unsatisfactory, but unrealistic.

In addition, our instructors are mindful of their existence in and obligations to the broader education community. Sensitive to the alarm being raised by policymakers and professional associations of an impending shortage in the principalship, it became necessary to examine educators' responsibility in crafting a resolution. Research being conducted on the subject has indicated that the looming crisis grows not from a lack of qualified applicants, but rather the increasingly unattractive dimensions of the job (Ferrandino & Tirozzi, 2000; Leary & Nicholson, 2000).

Among the unfavorable conditions cited by practicing principals (e.g., inadequate compensation, long work hours, increased pressure from policymakers and legislators, ongoing criticism, decreased public confidence) is one that calls into question the relevance of the preservice experience. Specifically, principals expressed dissatisfaction with curricula they considered "more theoretical than practical," saying they were left to learn many of the skills necessary to lead a school "by trial and error" (Leary & Nicholson, 2000, p. 210).

Taken together, these problems with the preservice experience clearly demonstrated a need for an alternative approach. What we did not see at the outset was that our initial interest in reforming the assessment practices would lead to a deeper pedagogical and epistemological understanding that would change the character of the entire preparation program.

That understanding, which confirms Donmoyer's (1995) suspicion that much of the knowledge we use is not specialized but serendipitous, leads us to believe that an interest in self-assessment can have a broad and powerful effect on both the entire preservice experience and subsequent practice. In particular, if we adhere to an understanding of epistemology as a constructivist process that conceives of individuals as the architects of their own knowledge, as opposed to one which conceives of them as passive objects waiting to be shaped by more knowledgeable beings, the potential of self-assessment to radically reform the preparation of professional administrators holds promise.

The chapters that follow focus on the various conceptual issues that have influenced our thinking, as well as the organizational framework that has been designed in an attempt to reconceive the preadministrative education program. What they will *not* do is present a prescriptive model for the redesign of educational leadership programs. Recommending this model as the most appropriate construct for others would presuppose the very uniformity that we have challenged.

Others can, however, adapt this model to their own needs, and in so doing expand the inquiry into the phenomenon of knowledge utilization as a measure of programmatic integrity. If that occurs, perhaps a contribution to meaningful curricular reform can be made. Thus, while this text will provide a foundation for students in our own program, it is our hope that faculty with an interest in what Schon (1987) identifies as "the elusive phenomena of practice competence . . . and the equally elusive processes by which these are acquired" (p. xiv) can find something valuable herein as well.

CHAPTER 1

Introduction

Why might a student in a preservice educational administration program find the development of a professional portfolio useful? For some, the primary rationale will be compliance with institutional requirements for obtaining their master's degrees. There are, however, other reasons to consider the beginning of a professional portfolio at the preservice stage, some functional, others more philosophical. This guide provides a step-by-step introduction to both the practical and theoretical elements involved in the development of the preservice principal portfolio (the P^3). Before turning to those chapters, however, the benefits of beginning the construction of a portfolio during the preservice phase of an administrative career merit some attention.

SELF-ASSESSMENT

Recent years have brought a number of challenges to the orthodoxy implicit in assessment rhetoric from kindergarten to postgraduate classrooms, their universal intent's being the improvement of public education. In higher education, this discourse has been energized by a variety of progressive approaches, among them an increasing acceptance of qualitative measures that are perhaps less authoritative but more illuminating than the quantitative measures that have dominated the field for literally decades. Among these approaches is portfolio assessment. The portfolio, while still presently used primarily in conjunction with some more conventional evaluation methods (e.g., comprehensive examinations, certification tests, performance appraisal instruments), has been gaining the support of both students and faculty across disciplines and has had a significant impact on teacher education programs (Darling-Hammond, Ancess, & Falk, 1995; Holmes Group, 1986; Lyons, 1998; Moss, 1997; National Board for Professional Teaching Standards, 1989; Schon, 1987; Schulman, 1988; Tierney, 1992).

The implementation of the portfolio as either an alternative or correlative assessment tool in educational leadership programs, however, has been less ubiquitous. This has been a puzzling phenomenon to some who work with preservice administrators, particularly in light of the body of research concerning the centrality of the principal's performance to school effectiveness. Despite what we know about the principal's integral role in various effectiveness measures, the majority of preservice administration programs have been characterized by the dubious premise that mastery of a prescribed knowledge base adequately prepares principals for the instrumental problems they will encounter in leadership practice. It is an approach that has not only divorced propositional knowledge (knowing *what*) from procedural knowledge (knowing *how*), but that has privileged the former to the virtual exclusion of the latter. The challenge for both those who teach and those enrolled in educational leadership programs is to reconcile these competing philosophies with an epistemological model that recognizes the value of both. The development of a preservice portfolio can help not only to effect that reconciliation, but to provide a foundation for the continued growth and development of the practicing administrator.

ESTABLISHING A REFLECTIVE PRACTICE

It is ironic that a discipline that at the beginning of the 20th century was exhorting its students to adopt what Murphy (1995a) calls "the captain of commerce role" (p. 63) is now witness to some of the better known management theorists' emphasizing business models predicated on educational premises. One of the more recognizable is Peter Drucker who, in 1989, was describing management as a liberal art: "Management is . . . 'liberal' because it deals with the fundamentals of knowledge, self-knowledge, wisdom, and leadership; 'art' because it is practice and application" (p. 231).

Unlike propositional knowledge, self-knowledge is not easily assessed in conventional ways. Sergiovanni (1995) argues that individuals aspiring to be effective principals need to know what they value, what they're committed to. It is this quality to which most refer when they employ the term "vision." Values, commitment, and vision, however, do not inhere in the content of a knowledge base, regardless of its breadth or depth. They grow in the spaces we carve out for ourselves to spend in contemplation when we begin to sense an incongruity between what we believe and what we're doing, in the friction of theory misaligned with practice. In the well-documented fragmentation of the principal's day, however, there's little time for this kind of reflection, what Schon (1987) calls "reflection-in-action" (p. 22).

Recognizing that the cultivation of a habit requires repetition, the P^3 is predicated on the premise that ongoing reflection, from the beginning of the student's program to the end, lays the groundwork for the extension of that behavior to professional practice. Underlying this premise is a constructivist foundation that identifies reflection as essential to the student's ability to continue to evolve as a self-directing, inquiring learner, and that recognizes lifelong learning as not only valuable, but imperative in a world where information with knowledge potential grows exponentially on a daily basis.

Neither information nor knowledge stands still. As information has accumulated, scholars have added to their knowledge bases in every discipline by making reasoned judgments concerning what constituted a valuable addition and what didn't. That task grows ever more difficult, however, as distinguishing what information is useful from what isn't, and determining how we've come to know that, gets increasingly complicated. That process is understood as constructivism, and reflection is its essential quality.

One becomes a lifelong learner through understanding, through awareness of the processes engaged in when he or she "comes to know." The identification of those processes is the product of thoughtful deliberation (i.e., reflection), which then "enhances [one's] ability to [continue to] learn and make sense of new information" (Lambert et al., 1995, p. 18). Schon (1983) argues that reflection is central to growth and development; that it is the ability to reflect on learning that allows students to construct the theoretical frameworks that will guide their practice. This awareness of the processes through which they have absorbed what they know imbues learning with a new character, making it dynamic, individually meaningful, and, most important, autonomous.

It is autonomy that separates constructivism as an epistemological construct from previous conceptions of how students learn. Previous epistemologies have for the most part construed students as beneficiaries in a sort of philanthropic relationship with their professors. Students came to "receive" the knowledge their professors "gave" to them, rendering them essentially passive participants in the learning process. As opposed to knowing subjects, they were cast as uninformed objects. Constructivist theory, however, consistent with Dewey's (1916) characterization of the student as a self-directed being, shifts the responsibility for learning from professor to student.

Embedded in that responsibility is the need for self-assessment. The more conventional forms of assessment (e.g., course, comprehensive, or licensing examinations), as Lambert et al. (1995) point out, "reinforce the notion that knowledge exists outside the student, and that the teacher's role is to transmit, and test the . . . acquisition of knowledge" (p. 24). Portfolio assessment, however, gives the student a pivotal role. It is a process characterized by a shift from what Chittenden and Gardner (1991) call a testing culture to an assessment culture—one in which assessment is continual and integrated, as opposed to transient and fragmentary. This shift represents a significant change in our understanding of assessment—one that is best facilitated not by a culminating examination, but by students' critical assessment of and reflection on the experiences they have as they prepare to become principals.

TRANSFORMING PEDAGOGY

The potential of the portfolio to resolve competing claims is not limited to epistemology, although its epistemological dimensions may be those of most benefit to the individual student. There are aspects to the use of the portfolio as a programmatic assessment tool that make its use valuable to institutions as well. Critical pedagogical issues for administrative preparation programs are frequently obscured, deliberately or not, by debates concerning academic questions of dubious importance.

Among those critical issues is the profound sense of dissatisfaction with contemporary educational administration programs that are characterized as being largely irrelevant and out of touch with practical concerns.

Murphy (1995a), in addressing the historical underpinnings of educational administration, believes we allowed that rift to develop out of deference to the persuasiveness of the scientific model and in response to the abuses of what he characterizes as the "prescriptive era" in the evolution of the knowledge base. The result, he argues, is this:

> Knowledge was something that was created at the university and applied in the field. It was a nonrecursive relationship. As a result of this academic self-conceit, a distinct breach developed between the university and field dimensions of the profession, one incorrectly and arrogantly labeled the theory–practice gap. The officially sanctioned knowledge base became increasingly less useful to practitioners. Worse yet, the processes and procedures employed to transmit this knowledge were often diametrically opposed to conditions that characterize the workplace in which school administrators found themselves. (p. 69)

Murphy's analysis is correct, of course, and that's a shame. It is a situation that is problematic for both the university professor who must necessarily concern him- or herself with the constraints of institutional support and the retention/promotion/tenure process, and for the student of administration who, having his or her graduate education reduced to an exercise in instrumentalism because certification requirements tend to force administrative preparation programs into a one-size-fits-all shape, resigns him- or herself to enduring hours of pointless study in the interest of getting a credential. Although there are always exceptions, such a circumstance would appear to be the rule. Were it not, we wouldn't continue to thrash about trying to find ways to ameliorate it.

Although a broad discussion of strategies for eliminating institutional constraints and the instrumental quality of certification requirements is beyond the scope and intent of this text, it is possible to examine the portfolio as one small reform that has the potential to at least mitigate their impact on the relationship between universities and schools as well as between faculties and students. If it is true, as Muth

(1995) believes, that "[u]sually reforms fail because they are not in the self-interest of those who could make them work" (p. 107), the portfolio has an excellent chance to succeed given the interests of all parties involved.

If it is the gap between university values and elementary and secondary schools' needs that keeps the two at cross-purposes, a mutual focus on the world of practice can serve to redefine the gap by making it common ground. If we reconceive of pedagogy not as the art or science of teaching but as lying at the intersection of teaching and learning, a discursive space wherein each informs the other, the potential of the portfolio to reform pedagogy begins to take shape. Supplemented by corresponding programmatic transformations (e.g., a redistribution of field experiences throughout the program accompanied by reflective entries developed in collaboration with field mentors and faculty), the portfolio can create multiple opportunities for a discursive relationship between universities and schools and between faculty and students that is pedagogically rewarding—one in which knowledge of what is useful in the world of practice can be jointly constructed. Students can play an integral role in that transformation.

IDENTIFYING POSTGRADUATE USES

The number of states that require portfolio evaluation for practicing administrators is growing. Given the number of accrediting agencies that now recommend the process, an increased interest on the part of state agencies that certify or license school administrators can be detected as well. Brown and Irby (1997) identify three potential reasons for the practicing principal to develop a professional portfolio: professional growth, evaluation, and career advancement:

> The first use of the portfolio, to encourage professional growth, emphasizes self-assessment and analysis of behaviors as they relate to the principal's performance. Because the major purpose is to determine areas in need of improvement, [it] is primarily for personal use and may or may not be shared with others. . . . The second use . . . is for summative evaluation. An external judgment of the effectiveness of the principal's leadership is made based on the artifacts and reflections included in the portfolio.

> Career advancement is the third use. . . . An innovative tool for pursuing leadership positions, seeking promotions, and assessing applicants, the artifacts and accompanying reflections represent strengths and accomplishments of the candidate that might not be apparent in the typical resume, application form or interview. (p. 2)

Whether one's future employer requires the development of a portfolio for evaluation or not, its potential to enhance personal growth and contribute to career advancement are compelling reasons to begin its development. Among the benefits cited to Brown and Irby (1997) by practicing administrators who had constructed portfolios were opportunities to reflect on their experiences by documenting their strengths, collecting evidence of their accomplishments, identifying their weaknesses, setting goals for improvement, and planning for their own professional development based on those goals (pp. 53–54). Leithwood and Montgomery (1986) suggest that the ability to reflect on this practice is central to an effective principalship, particularly as it relates to problem solving. Development of a preservice portfolio provides a foundation on which this kind of reflective practice can be established.

CAPITALIZING ON TECHNOLOGY

The choice to use an electronic format for portfolio construction has both a conceptual and a utilitarian rationale. As emerging technologies expand the dimensions of the classroom, demands that education professionals be familiar with not only their potential but their application increase as well. Because what is required of an individual to be technologically literate is something of a moving target, creating the portfolio in a constantly changing digital environment constitutes the kind of ongoing learning process encouraged by constructivist pedagogy. If it is the student's intent as he or she prepares for a position of leadership to develop an architectonic system that offers a means of resolving the kinds of problems he or she will encounter in practice, that teaches the student that part of critical thinking is making the connections between seemingly discrete pieces of information—constructing the portfolio in a digital environment provides an opportunity to learn to make and demonstrate that kind of (hyper)linking.

From a pragmatic perspective, the electronic format allows for portability and ease of handling; expedites editing; provides options that are either unavailable or awkwardly achieved in conventional portfolios (e.g., qualitative research can capitalize on video streaming, audio recording, and scanning documents as opposed to submitting reams of paper, and video and cassette tapes); includes a broad range of statistical packages for quantitative research; simplifies backup; and represents a kind of compact or easily accessible credential for potential employers as it can be committed to a Zip or compact disk, or loaded to a website. Needless to say, it also gives students a head start on the development of a system to document their professional growth as practitioners and to enhance their career advancement.

Such are the premises on which the preservice principal portfolio rests. They do not so much disclaim the value of a knowledge base as they resist its presumptuousness. Acquiring knowledge is one thing. Actualizing it is quite another. Emphasizing the former at the expense of the latter does only half the job of preparing students to be school administrators.

The chapters that follow will elaborate on the conceptual rationale underlying the preservice portfolio and will present a more detailed description of the developmental elements involved. Their primary intent is to guide students in the development of their own portfolios, but it is also hoped that they will help others who have an interest in the phenomenon of knowledge utilization as a measure of either professional competence or programmatic integrity. It is that phenomenon that provides the thematic unity for both the portfolio and this text.

CHAPTER 2

Epistemological Issues

A vigorous debate continues within the educational administration community concerning the appropriate preparation for preservice students. If it is true, as Prestine (1995) notes, that the trivialization of any given field by a single paradigmatic view is its greatest danger, then this debate surely signals the health of the discipline. Much of the discussion, or disagreement, revolves around the issue of whether a "knowledge base" for educational administrators can be said to exist.

PROPOSITIONAL VERSUS PROCEDURAL KNOWLEDGE

The licensing examination to which students must eventually submit is consistent with the traditional focus on transmitting an articulated body of knowledge that has characterized educational administration programs for many decades. There are, however, implicit dangers in an approach that essentially reduces administrative preparation to the acquisition of a set of facts and/or functions. Among them, as Prestine (1995) notes, is the assumption that comprehension or knowledge of these facts and/or functions necessarily translates into an ability to implement them in practice. "Domain knowledge," she argues, "by itself, provides insufficient clues for many students about how to actually use it in solving problems and carrying out tasks in practice" (p. 271). Prestine continues:

> [L]ittle has been said [by advocates of a structured knowledge base] about professional knowledge use; that is, about the knowledge that professionals actually use in their practice and, more importantly, about the

> ways in which they acquire and use such knowledge. Little if any consideration has been given to issues surrounding initial knowledge acquisition in preparation programs, the accessibility and use, nonuse, or modification of such knowledge in practice, and the contribution of such knowledge to the development of professional expertise. Yet, without such considerations, attempts to codify a knowledge base for educational administration are likely to be misdirected and misspent. (p. 271)

The even larger danger, she goes on to say, is that students may assume that what they are asked to learn in their courses is "the truth"; that having mastered the course content, they will believe that they know all there is to know. If it were, as she quips, once students have acquired all the "marbles" (i.e., course content), the game would be over. It is, of course, far from over. It is, in fact, just beginning. Educational leadership must be understood, as Prestine correctly suggests, as more than the sum of its curricular parts. The preparation program, which focuses exclusively on the acquisition of propositional or domain knowledge (i.e., on what to know), provides only part of the equation.

Acquisition, in other words, is not actualization. Schon (1987) characterizes this difference between propositional and procedural knowledge as a "rigor-or-relevance dilemma" (p. 8), although the mutual exclusivity of these concepts is not now and has never been imperative. The traditional administrative preparation program, however, with its customary comprehensive examination and need to prepare students for licensing tests, has clearly favored propositional knowledge.

It isn't that the acquisition of knowledge is not useful. Bloom (1987), D'Souza (1991), and Hirsch (1987) are not entirely wrong in their insistence on the pursuit of a discrete body of knowledge, and, as Glaser (1987) notes, "The performances of highly competent individuals indicate the possession of, rapid access to and efficient utilization of an organized body of . . . knowledge" (p. 82). Clearly it is difficult to investigate or even think about something unless something is known about it; and the pursuit of knowledge as an end in itself can certainly be satisfying, as philosophers since Plato have argued. There's nothing, however, pragmatic about it. Propositional knowledge is silent on the matter of how it can be transformed in a generative way, how it can be "efficiently used" to resolve the more mundane, "commonplace" dilemmas, as Aristotle characterized them, we face on a daily basis. Acquisition is the first step to knowledge construction, not the last.

The epistemological model best suited to that transformation is constructivism. A primary principle of constructivist learning theory is that we learn by actively constructing knowledge, by comparing new information with our prior understandings, and by reflecting on and resolving discrepancies between the two to either alter or reinforce both our theoretical positions and subsequently our practices. It is not an accumulative process; rather, it asks us to reflect and reconceptualize. Propositional knowledge is transformed when we learn how to question, analyze, and synthesize it in a meaningful way so it can be put to practical use.

Identifying what it is that needs to be known in order to claim mastery of a particular discipline is one matter that Prestine (1995) calls a "well-structured domain" (p. 273). Well-structured domains are characterized by a formal, decontextualized, static body of knowledge that need not be transferred or applied outside of the domain. Math and science fields are prime examples, consisting of what she refers to as "prepackaged knowledge structures" for which there is little opportunity or even need for adaptation in other contexts.

Understanding what needs to be known in what is characterized as an "ill-structured domain" (Prestine, 1995, p. 273), however, is quite another matter. In an ill-structured domain, the lack of predictable or well-defined problems defies the a priori identification of appropriate knowledge. The contexts in which knowledge in an ill-structured domain will have to be put to use are so unique and situation-specific that it is impossible to anticipate all of them in advance. Consider this metaphor from Schon (1987):

> In the varied topography of professional practice, there is a high, hard ground overlooking a swamp. On the high ground, manageable problems lend themselves to solution through the application of research-based theory and technique. In the swampy lowland, messy, confusing problems defy technical solution. The irony of this situation is that the problems of the high ground tend to be relatively unimportant to individuals or society at large, however great their technical interest may be, while in the swamp lie the problems of greatest human concern. The practitioner must

> choose. Shall he remain on the high ground where he can solve relatively unimportant problems according to prevailing standards of rigor, or shall he descend to the swamp of important problems? (p. 3)

Acknowledging that a career in public education is the equivalent of working in the swamp presents some difficulties as it relates to proper preparation. If it is true, as Schon goes on to argue, that this is an area of "unfamiliar situations where the problems are not clear and there is no obvious fit between the characteristics of the situation and the available body of [knowledge]" (p. 34), then how is one to identify what it is necessary to know? It is a particularly vexing question in professions that involve both external certification and internal validation:

> One of the problems encountered in any discussion of knowledge or knowledge base is that both terms refer to something external as well as to something internal. On the one hand, the terms . . . connote an identifiable, durable intellectual framework of a domain. . . . On the other hand, knowledge and a knowledge base can be conceptualized as internalized phenomena that are experienced, understood, and constructed in different ways by different individuals. This constructivist understanding is crucial, in that it posits that knowledge can only be understood by the individual as it is constructed by the [individual's] mind. (Prestine, 1995, pp. 278–279)

It is this kind of experiential learning on which the portfolio is predicated. The documentation of students' experiences, both curricular and cocurricular, throughout their preparation can provide opportunities for their transforming propositional knowledge into procedural knowledge. As Prestine concludes, the usefulness of any given "knowledge base" will rest "less on its presumed validity than on the ability and willingness of people to use it" (p. 278). Although many education reformers consider the portfolio idea a novel one, the claim that there should be a relationship between thought and action traces its origins to the classical period.

THE THOUGHT–ACTION DICHOTOMY: A "CELIBACY OF INTELLECT"

Many of the metaphysical debates between Plato and his student Aristotle centered on the varied distinctions between philosophy and rhetorical theory. Although Aristotle shared his mentor's reverence for human knowledge, derived through the syllogistic properties of the dialectical process, it was his sentiment that the full value of knowledge is realized only when it is applied in the broader realm of human affairs. It was not the philosophical but the rhetorical syllogism, which Aristotle termed the "enthymeme," that allowed for such realization. The syllogistic equation was the same in both cases (i.e., if A = B, and B = C, then A = C). The difference was that Plato's dialectical syllogism resulted, he believed, in what was true. Aristotle's rhetorical syllogism, practiced in pragmatic rather than philosophical circumstances, resulted in what was *probably* true. Its result, as Brumbaugh (1981) describes it, "was not new knowledge, but action" (p. 187).

The persuasiveness of the argument that human affairs did not lend themselves to processes laying claim to absolute truth resulted in the general acceptance of the Aristotelian "canon," combining thought and action, as the foundation of Western thought and education for several centuries. It wasn't until the 16th century, nearly 2,000 years later, that the connection was broken in Peter Ramus's "Whatever Aristotle Has Said Is a Fabrication"(as cited in Dawson, n. d.). A professor of philosophy in the College de France, Ramus was a prolific writer publishing some five dozen works ranging from physics to epistemology. It was his interest in the latter, and his belief that the canon complicated rather than simplified learning, that led to the eventual demise of interdisciplinarity in the academy.

Ramus's epistemological theory, informed more by utility than perception, was grounded in compartmentalization. His general disdain for Aristotle led him to reduce rhetoric to mere oratorical style and delivery, thus rendering it the sole province of professors of eloquence. This conception of rhetoric as discursive ornamentation as opposed to a means for bringing knowledge to bear on human problems not only robbed it of its stature, but led to the convention of academic specializations that characterizes the educational enterprise to this day. "Fields" were identified, and "disciplines" within those fields. Buildings were constructed to facilitate the isolation of those fields and disciplines, and incoming students were asked to declare what precisely they wanted to study and thus to choose where they would be spending the bulk of their time. Research was separated from teaching, and research and teaching from public service. Soon entire campuses would take on designations as research or teaching institutions, and both the students and faculty in them would develop a remarkable inability to discern any interrelationships between and among their courses and, even worse, between their studies and their subsequent practice.

Although perhaps unaware that it is the Ramistic principle against which they inveigh (since such knowledge is, after all, specialized), many have challenged the compartmentalization of higher education and its corresponding divorce of thought from action. As long ago as 1916, Bailey, whose work explicitly connected higher education and civic activism and influenced the development of the national Cooperative Extension Service, questioned the isolation of the academy from public life: "What is the purpose and what the value of our widespread teaching . . . if not that its mental attitude is to be applied in all the horizons of life?" (p. 22).

Bailey's sentiments were echoed by Harding (as cited in Peters, Jordan, & Lemme, 1999), a scientist who was the editor of scientific publications for the U.S. Department of Agriculture. Harding criticized what he considered a "prevailing professional culture in science" in an essay titled "Science and Agricultural Policy," in which he addressed the tendency of scientists in the academy to isolate themselves and argued that "rigid compartmentalization [had] sterilize[d] scientific knowledge by depriving scientific specialists of broad social vision":

> [F]ew scientific specialists have progressive, intelligent opinions in fields outside their speciality. Very often they even lack the ability to express the results of their work in such a manner as to contribute to the normal life and growth of the community. A celibacy of intellect has characterized scientists that resembles the physical celibacy practiced by the learned of the Middle Ages. (p. 1103)

Although it may be supposed that scientists, owing to their centuries of dedication to logical positivism, are more likely to fall victim to the charge that they are disconnected from human affairs, scholars in other fields have also been enlisted in the search for a way to restore a sense of unity to the pursuit of higher knowledge that connects it to practice in their own disciplines. Lanham (1993), in an examination of the effects of technology on the teaching of rhetorical theory, raises what he calls "the Q question" in honor of its "most famous nonanswerer,"

Quintilian (p. 155). The question concerns the need for humanists to demonstrate a connection between humanistic study and civic responsibility, between what they know and what they do.

McCloskey (1985) actually explores the Ramistic separation of philosophy and rhetoric, or thought and action, which he sees as responsible for what he describes as the "modernist, objectivist" style of teaching economics (p. 178). It should not be surprising, he suggests, that students who have been taught various discrete theories that purport to explain certain economic phenomena are unable to reconcile those theories with practical problems that arise outside the classroom. Expertise in economic theory is insufficient preparation for addressing contemporary multifaceted questions that require an understanding of history, sociology, and politics, among other things.

In the field of educational leadership as well, Murphy (1995a) identifies a number of initiatives under way to "ground pre-service administrative programs in the world of practice and to anchor scholarship in the problems of the field." He considers such efforts hopeful indications that an attempt to "re-legitimize the craft aspects of the profession" is under way (p. 69). The publication of *The Knowledge Base in Educational Administration: Multiple Perspectives* (Donmoyer, Imber, & Scheurich, 1995), which is a book-length challenge to the claim that a knowledge base can even be said to exist in educational administration, is evidence of that attempt.

The value of the rhetorical tradition of connecting thought and action is not merely that it provides students the opportunity to wander at will through multiple subjects, but that it emphasizes their interrelationships. If students have no experience in examining the overall coherence of their previous programs of study, in integrating what they think with what they do, it is necessarily difficult to see those interrelationships. Institutional reliance on the Ramistic principle has encouraged precisely the opposite. Cultivating an ability to integrate what students have learned is rooted in yet another Aristotelian concept—"theoria," or reflection. It is reflection, he believed, that allows us to integrate seemingly discrete pieces of information into a more holistic thought pattern that can then inform our actions. It would seem to be self-evident, however, that such a process requires time; and time is a scarce commodity for principals.

THE PRINCIPAL'S NEED FOR REFLECTION

The research devoted to how principals spend their time substantiates the need for reflection. There is a wealth of data related to the myriad responsibilities of the principal (Barth, 1990; Bossert, Dwyer, Rowan, & Lee, 1982; Fullan, 1988; Leithwood & Jantzi, 1990; Leithwood & Montgomery, 1986; Manasse, 1985; Smith & Andrews, 1989) and to her or his role in school effectiveness (Anderson, 1989; Brookover, 1981; Edmonds, 1979; Hall, 1988; Lezotte et al., 1980; Louis & Miles, 1990; Marsh, 1988; Mortimer et al., 1988; Teddlie, Kirby, & Stringfield, 1989). Research related to how principals actually spend their time, however, indicates that these roles and responsibilities are often subordinated to other demands on their time.

A benchmark study conducted by anthropologist Harry Wolcott (1973) found that virtually all of the principal's time was given to one-on-one personal encounters, meetings, and telephone calls. Martin and Willower (1981) confirmed Wolcott's findings, describing the principal's workday as one filled with disruptions characterized by their brief and fragmented nature. They reported that the average secondary principal performs an average of 149 tasks a day, that those activities are exceedingly brief (84% taking only 1 to 4 minutes) and that over 59% of the activities are interrupted. The principals they observed "demonstrated a tendency to engage themselves in the most current and pressing situation[s]," and "invested little time in reflective planning" (p. 80).

Peterson (1981) and Sarason (1982) also observed that most of the principal's day is spent on administrative housekeeping matters and maintaining order, as did House and Lapan (1978):

> The principal has no set of priorities except to keep small problems from becoming big ones. His is a continuous task of crisis management. He responds to emergencies daily. He is always on call. All problems are seen as important. This global response to any and all concerns means he never has the time, energy, or inclination to develop or carry out a set of premeditated plans of his own. Containment of all problems is his theme. (p. 145)

A longitudinal project conducted by Crowson and Porter-Gehrie (1980) cited maintenance as the primary characteristic of the principal's day as well, mentioning specifically student discipline, dealing with outside influences (e.g., the board of education, parents, business leaders), negotiating staff conflicts, and ensuring the school has adequate material resources and staff on hand.

Edu-con's 1984 study of 137 principals and vice principals revealed that 90% of those surveyed reported an increase over the previous 5 years in the demands made on their time, and that 61% felt these increased demands had reduced their effectiveness. Ninety-one percent said "no" when asked "Do you think the principal can effectively fulfill all the responsibilities assigned to him/her?" Their feelings may be summed up by a respondent to interviews conducted by Duke (1988) who was talking with principals concerning their pending resignations: "The conflict for me comes from going home every night acutely aware of what didn't get done and feeling after six years that I ought to have a better batting average than I have" (p. 309).

Although Duke's qualitative analysis features a small sample, the comments of the interviewees are wholly consistent with the findings of similar research studies. The majority reflects the summation offered by Cuban (1988), who conducted a meta-analysis of studies spanning a 70-year period examining the role of the principal. The earliest reported study, in 1910, featured essentially the same finding as those detailed above: "While styles differ, the managerial role . . . has dominated principals' behavior" (Cuban, 1988, p. 84). Ferrandino (2001), in examining the U.S. Department of Labor's report that 40% of the nation's 93,200 principals are nearing retirement and that the need for school leaders can be expected to increase by 10 to 20% by 2006, characterizes the problem as one of principals' being "encumbered by bureaucratic minutiae" (p. 72).

What follows? Is it that, given the constraints imposed by school systems, it is impossible for principals to engage in thoughtful leadership? That, given the circumstances, we can expect little of them other than to reel from task to task intent on merely keeping order? No. Not that it is impossible; merely that it is difficult. To reach any other conclusion is to credit the system with more influence than it merits. Although systemic elements can certainly influence our performances, as Sarason notes (1982), " 'the system' is frequently conceived by the individual in a way that obscures, many times *unwittingly*, the range of possibilities available to him or her" (p. 164, emphasis added).

What is necessary, then, for the principal to become aware that limitations perceived to be imposed by the system might, in fact, be self-imposed? A consciousness of one's autonomy, achieved through continuous introspection.

WHY THE PORTFOLIO?

What kind of epistemological model, providing opportunities consistent with reflection and constructivism, might be most appropriate for preservice professionals? Searches under the subject of assessment using the terms "reflection" and "constructivism" return repeated references to the same approach: the portfolio. Portfolios, which have been considered standard in such fields as art and architecture, are becoming ubiquitous in teacher education programs as well, and have migrated from classrooms to state departments of education and accrediting bodies. They are presently the primary means of assessment employed by the National Board for Professional Teaching Standards for certification of experienced teachers, and are under consideration by the Interstate New Teacher Assessment and Support Consortium for licensing new teachers (Lyons, 1998). Both the National Council for the Accreditation of Teacher Education and the Interstate School Leaders Licensure Consortium are considering their implementation for those purposes as well.

THE CENTRALITY OF REFLECTION

Since portfolio assessment made its appearance in teacher education programs only in the 1980s, there is not yet a solid research base to document their long-term consequences. Studies in the various arenas where portfolios have been introduced, however, have demonstrated their congruence with the value of reflection. Lyons (1998) reports that one of the benefits of engaging in the development of a portfolio is "the power of the opportunity for reflection." Although veteran and novice teachers appear to experience some degree of differences in the meaning of the experience, "all report that the process helps them to identify for themselves the critical features of their own . . . platforms and philosophies" (p. 248). She goes on to point out, as do others (Freidus, 1996; LaBoskey, 1994, 1996), that novice or intern teachers reported a direct connection between reflection and their actual teaching and work with students:

> One teacher intern revealed the way her portfolio learning . . . became a part of her teaching practices during her internship year. Seeing that the portfolio process "made me think about my purpose . . . made me probe deeper . . . what is the driving purpose? what is it that you want to accomplish? and what purpose does it have? is it useful?" She found the process continued into her internship: "When I prepare a lesson plan or am asked to do something with the children, I constantly ask myself: What do I want the kids to get out of this? Why? Why am I doing this? So in that sense it was really beneficial. And I try to think of that as I go through this whole process [of learning to teach]." (pp. 248–249, brackets in original)

It is this kind of consciousness of practice that is important as students "go through this whole process" of learning to be school leaders. Such consciousness, however, should not be presumed as a condition of the graduate experience. It should not, in fact, be presumed as a condition of professional practice. Many professors, themselves products of a professional culture that requires only sporadic self-examination, fail to train a conscious eye on their work until required to prepare tenure reviews or annual reports; and even then, the objective is less personal growth than professional advancement.

The creation of a portfolio addresses that presumption. By documenting both their work and their thinking about their work as they co-evolve, students have an opportunity to develop the kind of sustained reflection that should be a condition of their graduate experience and their lives as professionals. Conditioning themselves to engage in critical self-examination on an ongoing basis contributes to their internalizing the process, to believing in its importance to their continued professional growth.

It should be noted that the acceptance of reflection as vital to professional practice has not gone unchallenged. Ecclestone (1996) worries that there has been insufficient critical analysis concerning reflection, and calls on its proponents to "offer . . . clearer accounts of different interpretations and values which underpin reflection and to structure its forms and focuses more coherently" (p. 152). Bleakley (1999) agrees and undertakes to conduct "a rigorous inquiry into the 'notion' of reflection" (p. 316). His examination, however, yields not an indictment of the "notion," but a recommendation for a third form of the practice.

Arguing that reflection is not a unitary phenomenon, Schon (1987) draws a distinction between reflection-on-action, which is retrospective, and reflection-in-action, where thinking and doing coincide. Reflection-*on*-action is engaged when one pauses to consider a phenomenon after it has occurred, examining the implications or consequences, his or her role in them, and so forth. Reflection-*in*-action, on the other hand, is intuitive, grounded in a deeper knowledge that allows one to respond to an unexpected circumstance in an appropriate fashion. Bleakley (1999) suggests that this understanding is grounded in Polanyi's (1996) model of "tacit knowing" (i.e., that we know more than we can say or bring to our immediate awareness).

Bleakley (1999) proposes a third form, "reflection-*as*-action" (p. 322), which he offers as a challenge to "the rational Enlightenment view that frames reflection as the ability for the human mind to think about its own thinking" (p. 324). He conceives of this third form as embedded in the philosophical framework of radical phenomenology, a locus he describes as post-Heideggerean and one in which the "locus for reflection is not 'in' the individual (decontextualised), but 'in' the total event" (p. 323). By grounding the reflective act in a context that itself shapes the act, Bleakley is then able to frame it as an aesthetic rather than a cognitive process.

Bleakley's argument for elevating reflection to the aesthetic level, however sophisticated and interesting, appears to rest on an assumption that the Enlightenment view to which he objects is the norm; that individuals do, in fact, routinely think about their own thinking. Such reflection, however, as Bolin (1988) notes, is not a given of the human condition. Bleakley's argument for a third form is valuable, however, in that it more closely conforms to the reflective quality contemporary scholars consider important, be it cognitive or aesthetic.

THE ASSESSMENT ROLE

In her characterization of the portfolio as the manifestation of a new professionalism, Lyons (1998) points out that teaching has, "for more than a century . . . viewed the teacher as the occupant of a role, subject to the rules of a bureaucracy" (p. 13). Like teaching, school administration has also been thought of primarily as an occupation. Like the teacher, the principal occupies a role, laboring under the regulations of a bureaucracy. And like teachers, principals have experienced evaluation or assessment, as Lyons notes, as something done *to* them. In an environment in which assessment has been administered almost exclusively as external evaluation, primarily in the form of tests, that perception should come as no surprise.

The portfolio model transforms that process. It is students rather than external evaluators who will stand at the center of portfolio assessment. They'll gather, document, and select evidence of their work, authored by them and accompanied by their reflective evaluations of it, to explain how that work has shaped their perceptions and their practice. Going beyond the content knowledge that characterizes licensing examinations, the portfolio allows them to assess their own growth and development by articulating their thoughts on such issues as vision, integrity, or judgment. They can explore how those viewpoints were derived (i.e., how they have come to know what they know).

That exploration will permit them to acknowledge another element, of equal or even more importance, that content exams reject as valuable: their mistakes. Snyder, Lippincott, and Bower (1998) call them "the bombs," and quote one of their students on their relevance:

> I kept the bombs. . . . I had to look at what I did . . . good and bad. . . . I tried to find [the entries] that were bombs and the ones that were good to compare and contrast. . . . [R]ather than saying, 'Show your competencies,' it was 'Show your growth in this area.' . . . The purpose is not to show perfection in any of these things; it is to show your change in practice and thinking over time. (p. 133)

When students can conceive of their mistakes as potentially constructive, as an integral part of their learning process, they can begin to discern the flaw in one of the great fallacies embraced by educators at virtually every stage of their professional development: that not knowing is a failure. What veteran educators know is that no one has all the answers and that not knowing, in situations that call for judgment as opposed to a multiple-choice response, is, in fact, a typical condition. Owning their mistakes, having the latitude to be imperfect and to explore what was learned through that imperfection, gives them an opportunity no content examination can provide.

Because professional growth occurs in circumstances other than those that are related solely to students' academic programs, the development of a portfolio also provides a place for students to gather evidence of their learning in other environments. Conventions or annual meetings of professional organizations, faculty or staff development workshops, grant-writing experiences, presentations to policymaking bodies, committee work, participation in civic organizations, parent–teacher conferences, and preparation of articles for publication all constitute potentially valuable experiences they may wish to document. They may wish to keep track as well of performance evaluations, any honors, awards, or commendations, and an updated version of their vitae.

Understanding that valuable learning takes place in collaborative circumstances as well as in solitary reflection, the preservice principal portfolio permits opportunities for ongoing assessment with peers, faculty, and external mentors. The program of study includes two courses in which portfolio development is the primary focus, featuring peer reviews; periodic formative evaluations undertaken with individual faculty members; experiential learning opportunities supervised and evaluated by field mentors, who also review folios-in-progress; and a collaborative capstone experience. This final step, grounded in the work of Vygotsky (1978) and Bruner (1994) who argue that we come to know ourselves primarily through our interactions with others, is a public seminar in which students present the completed portfolio. The setting is designed to engage students, faculty, peers, and mentors in a collaborative inquiry that ultimately invites all participants to revisit their own leadership philosophies, the goal of which is to internalize the explaining, elaborating, and interrogating of our respective understandings in a learning community as an ongoing element of professional practice. All are predicated on the premise that the process of reflection is both private and public, and that it is the latter wherein students may learn the most about the values they have and how they have developed them.

In addition to their relationships with their field mentors, students are encouraged to establish a support group of their peers who will agree to provide feedback concerning their work and professional growth and the degree to which their portfolios adequately represent them. Although these support/cohort groups tend to evolve naturally during students' matriculation, it is strongly recommended that they begin to establish a network.

Finally, a word about validity. Although the issue will be examined in more detail in the epilogue, it is important at this point to note that as new forms of assessment are implemented, former measures for determining validity will likely be found insufficient. The four primary measures—concurrent validity, predictive validity, content validity, and construct validity—are, as Schulman (1998) observes, too limited in the case of validating portfolios. He argues for a fifth form—consequential or systemic validity—offering this rationale:

> The claim that some form of assessment is valid requires that you offer evidence that when you deploy it, it has positive consequences for the entire system of which it is a part. The assessment cannot merely discriminate reliably, or correlate with some other indicator. In terms of teacher assessment, this new requirement means that any form of teacher assessment has to meet a new standard: that the manner in which it is deployed improves the quality of teaching and opportunities for becoming a better teacher. That's consequential validity for teacher assessment. (p. 30)

It is hoped that the preservice principal portfolio can be deployed in a way that improves the quality of educational leadership. The primary interest is not whether such a project enhances the professionalism of graduates as it relates to their credentials. Should such a circumstance emerge, it should be understood as more a byproduct of the project than its goal. The intent is to create a process that is founded on knowledge utilization; on providing access to knowledge and ample opportunity to actualize it in a way that is useful in the world of practice. If "portfolio principals" believe they have achieved that goal, the criterion of consequential validity will have been met.

CHAPTER 3

Conceptual Framework

There is a certain truth to the maxim that advises that if we don't care where we are going, any destination is okay. If, however, we *do* care, the choice of destination is crucial. If we intend for our students to be autonomous, to develop the intellectual discipline they will require to become lifelong learners, it is important to recognize the deep impact the creation of a portfolio can have. If self-assessment is to be understood as a process, its presence will need to be discernible from the beginning of the student's portfolio construction to the end. What is needed is a framework that will not only provide a scaffolding for the development of the portfolio, but which will convey an element of literacy to the project itself.

Literacy, of course, connotes more than an ability to read and write. It is also, as those who have labored to deepen the appreciation of minorities' histories perceive, a way of developing and maintaining a perspective that originates from within, a worldview that is informed by the understandings and experiences of one's own kind. Poet Nikki Giovanni's (as cited in Harris, 1999) emphasis on the importance of literacy reflects this understanding, as does George Santayana's much earlier observation that those who are unaware of their history are doomed to repeat it. Giovanni, writing a mere decade after the turbulence of the civil rights movement and as the women's movement was gathering steam, sought to reduce the observation to a more personal level. Hers was an understanding that freedom in the broadest sense is secured by knowledge in the smallest—in the individual. Literate individuals know themselves and their histories, and value both. Theirs is a perspective imposed not by external authority, but by internal consciousness.

The field of educational leadership is not, of course, analogous to the struggle endured by countless human beings for freedom and dignity the world over. Yet to the extent that we have devalued the rich and varied experiences that individuals bring to the practice of administration by imposing one set of standards or another in an effort to ensure conformity to a preconceived knowledge base, we too have privileged external knowledge. The discourse concerning assessment of student outcomes, however, is becoming more expansive. From kindergarten to university, conventional assessment rhetoric has been amplified by an increasing recognition that those attributes thought necessary to evaluate include not only universal content knowledge, but individual qualities such as judgment, motivation, and integrity; intellectual skills such as critical thinking and problem analysis; and dispositions for engaging in such practices as collaboration or lifelong learning.

ASSESSING COMPLEXITIES

Clearly the development of an assessment instrument that can adequately capture these kinds of complexities in any kind of uniform fashion eludes us, as it has eluded those who prepare teachers. Schon (1987) argues that the reason for this deficiency is that conversations about standards and performance appraisals that focus solely on outcomes, absent any clarification of the conception of teaching or learning they embody, simply miss the mark. Lyons (1998), in an examination of teacher certification examinations, describes the problem:

> Consisting largely of multiple choice questions and writing samples, and sometimes including descriptions of brief teaching scenarios for which one selected a correct answer, teaching tests were denounced for their failure to measure adequately or accurately actual teaching performance. (p. 13)

If the new professionalism is to take into account standards of practice as well as standards of content knowledge, those standards and methods of assessing them will have to be developed. Although the National Board for Professional Teaching Standards (1989) concedes that "even state-of-the-art assessments probably cannot fully capture teaching's complexities" (p. 11), the search for an instrument that could at least address those complexities led them to the Stanford Teaching Assessment Project and portfolios. Schulman (1998), who designed the project after a model he created for the Institute for Research on Teaching at Michigan State University, explains why:

> [W]hen we created the Institute, we designed it as a powerful argument against the prevailing views of teaching as skilled behavior—the process–product conception of teaching. . . . We argued then that teaching was a form of thought and judgment, that it was an act of an autonomous agent engaged in creating opportunities for students and adapting all kinds of goals and materials to the conditions of the moment and the students taught. (p. 24)

Educational leadership too resists the "process–product" characterization. As surely as schools need skilled teachers who are not only knowledgeable but committed to students and to maintaining "professional standards of practice and ethics" (Darling-Hammond, 1988, p. 12), they need administrators whose knowledgeability, commitment, and professionalism are equally ensured. If a central aspiration of the portfolio is to challenge that process–product orientation by conceiving of preservice teacher education as more than the accumulation of course credits and content knowledge, it offers opportunities for the reconceptualization of preservice administrative education as well.

There will always be accrediting bodies to administer tests. So long as those preparing educational leaders operate within a framework of choice, however, students' preparation need not be limited to the propositional knowledge assessed by licensing agencies or by the tradition of comprehensive examinations. If we who are preparing principals believe school leaders should possess both propositional and procedural knowledge, and that the proper role of educational leadership programs is to ensure that they have the opportunity to not only acquire the former, but actualize the latter, the potential of the portfolio approach holds promise. That promise, however, can be realized only if both are made explicit.

WHICH PRINCIPLES FOR PRINCIPALS?

The portfolio, because it is student-centered, brings us closer to a form of assessment that is truly "authentic," that is, "measuring the real, actual or genuine" (Case, 1992, p. 19), than does any previous instrument. The construction of the portfolio gives students a broader opportunity to not only demonstrate some of the attributes that more conventional assessment instruments find immeasurable, but to do so in a way that enhances their internal consciousness of practice (i.e., their administrative literacy). But what are the proper attributes? They will, necessarily, vary according to students' own inclinations and program priorities.

The literature focusing on the reform of educational leadership programs reflects three central themes, distilled by Murphy (1995b): "1) defining and sustaining educational purpose; 2) developing and nurturing community; and 3) fostering personal and organizational growth" (p. 2). Clark and Clark (1996) see in these themes an emphasis on "mission, shared vision, webs of communication, breaking down of hierarchies, shared governance, personal development, lifelong learning, and learning communities" (p. 18). Carlson (1996) suggests that what is needed is "leaders and followers invested in a transformational process" (p. 137). Yerkes (1995) has a more pragmatic list, including "instructional leadership; manag[ing] a variety of programs; deal[ing] with social issues from teen pregnancy to violence; work[ing] with parents from a multitude of language groups; and keep[ing] students, staff and community focused on improving learning for students" (p. 10).

Although ultimately there are sufficient commonalities among these themes, preservice students beginning the preparation of portfolios will require a more explicit set of principles that can serve as an organizational framework. Taking into account the themes that inhere in the research, the reports of the various accrediting agencies, the policies of regulatory bodies such as state departments of education and legislatures, and the observations of practicing administrators, it is possible to identify six attributes most consider vital to effective educational leadership: (1) emphasis of the significance of vision; (2) expression of the importance of learning, principals' own as well as their students' and teachers'; (3) addressing of the role of the administrator as trustee of the school's resources; (4) stressing of the value of collaboration with multiple constituencies; (5) assertion of the centrality of integrity to the practice of leadership; and (6) acknowledgement of the larger social, political, and cultural contexts in which the school functions.

Leadership, like any other human endeavor, emerges from one's intrinsic qualities. Students' ongoing reflection can make these principals part of those qualities they bring to their schools. There remains, however, the practical issue of ensuring that they have access as well to the propositional knowledge assessed through licensing examinations. Regardless of the contestability of the claim that a universal knowledge base exists, agencies that certify and/or license school administrators require that those who would be principals submit to an examination grounded in one set of standards or another. The next question, then, is whether these principles can be said to conform to the standards on which various licensing agencies rely.

WHICH STANDARDS?

The Elusiveness of the Knowledge Base

Diverse intellectual perspectives such as feminism, critical theory, postmodernism, and so forth have illuminated both epistemological and pedagogical problems with the idea of an accepted knowledge base in educational administration (i.e., Which is the "correct" knowledge base, if there is one? Are accepted knowledge bases out of touch with the instrumental issues school administrators have to face?). Assuming the existence of such a knowledge base has, according to Scheurich (1995), a dual function: it affirms to those outside the field that there is a body of knowledge and skills its practitioners are required to master, and it standardizes the preparation necessary for practitioners in such a way that, within a range of acceptable variations, it makes little difference which institution provides the preparation (pp. 17–18). Every graduate, thus, regardless of institutional preparation, would theoretically possess a common body of knowledge.

The question, of course, is whether there *is* such a common body of knowledge. Clearly, various accrediting bodies and professional organizations believe it exists. The National Policy Board for Educational Administration (1989), the University Council for Educational Administration (1992), and the Interstate School Leaders Licensure Consortium (1996) have all drafted documents articulating various content standards predicated on the work of scholars such as Culbertson (1988), who argues that "there is an extensive body of knowledge available for use" in the field (p. 23). Studies by Griffiths (1988a) and Nicolaides and Gaynor (1989), examining textbook usage in educational administration, confirm the appearance of such a knowledge base, but point out that it is largely positivist or structuralist/functionalist. Such observations raise the obvious concern that the effect of articulating such a body of knowledge as standard would be to limit the field to what Scheurich (1995) and others (Bredeson, 1995; Littrell & Foster, 1995; Sanford, 1995; Shakeshaft, 1995) see as the same conventional orientation that has characterized it for decades.

Schon (1987), in fact, argues that any such construct as a "knowledge base" can be derived from and is operational only in relationship to the positivist archetype, which he refers to as "technical rationality." Other scholars agree (Smith & Heshusius, 1986; Sparkes, 1989) and assert further a fundamental incongruity between and among all archetypes, so that any body of knowledge grounded in one will be necessarily incompatible with any other. Scheurich (1995) explains why:

> They assume different views of humans; they assume different views of the appropriate methods for inquiry; they assume different positions in terms of what reality itself is. A body of knowledge derived from one of these paradigms will, thus, not fit within the theoretical suppositions of another paradigm. (p. 20)

The notion of fundamental incompatibility, however, has been challenged by others, among them Gage (1989) and Howe and Eisenhart (1990), who argue that although there may be epistemological incongruities at the philosophical level, at the practical level the tension between and among disparate perspectives can be ameliorated by considering them complementary approaches. Scheurich (1995) concedes that such a position has a "certain compelling logic to it" (p. 20) and that, in certain circumstances (e.g., combining the interpretivist and functionalist approaches in the study of a particular organization), it may have some potential. He goes on to conclude, however, that the distance between certain axiological stances renders any argument for their complementarity difficult, if not impossible.

Such disagreement among scholars in the field illuminates the difficulty of discerning consensus on a knowledge base for educational administrators. The issue is further complicated by state or district reliance on examinations conforming to the expectations of the respective accrediting agency by whom they are regulated. Since it cannot be presumed that a student will seek licensure in only one locale, given the possibility or even likelihood of professional mobility, the multiplicity of accrediting agencies and the corresponding diversity of their standards must be taken into consideration.

Making the Choice

The recent efforts by accrediting agencies to standardize a knowledge base are broader than their predecessors. Some, in fact, such as those developed by the National Policy Board for Educational Administration (1989) and the Interstate School Leaders Licensure Consortium (1996) encompass many of the concerns of postpositivists, such as the acceptance of qualitative research methods, the systematic questioning of prevailing assumptions, the demographics of educational administration, and the value of theoretical pluralism. The pragmatic difficulties students would face, however, in attempting to develop a portfolio that would address all of the standards of the multiple accrediting agencies would be overwhelming. That being the case, the question is whether there exists a set of standards that essentially conforms to the basic themes that inhere in the various reform efforts. Is there, among the proposed sets of standards, one that is universal, one that subsumes the concerns common to all of them?

The standards proposed by the Interstate School Leaders Licensure Consortium (ISLLC) appear to best correlate with the themes articulated above and can be recommended as one appropriate framework for construction of the portfolio. The standards developed by ISLLC (which is affiliated with the Council of Chief State School Officers [CCSSO]), have, in fact, been confirmed by both the National Council on the Accreditation of Teacher Education (NCATE) and the National Policy Board for Educational Administration (NPBEA) as congruent with their own:

> While the ISLLC Standards and Indicators and the NPBEA and national NCATE Curriculum Guidelines were developed primarily by separate participants, it was the joint goal of the NPBEA and the CCSSO to maintain congruence between the two efforts so that similar knowledge, skills and attributes were reflected in both final products as is typical with other professions. . . . These commonalities reflect the qualities common

to other major professions and provide a unified foundation for the field of educational leadership. (Murphy, Shipman, & Thomson, 1996, p. 2)

Students who developed portfolios as part of a joint venture between a local school district and two Texas universities designed to recruit administrative candidates reported that using the structural framework of an articulated body of standards was helpful in the construction process. They found that having the 21 dimensions suggested by the National Policy Board for Educational Administration around which to build their portfolios helped them move from the abstract idea of assessment to the concrete reality of choosing what to include. Some observed that organizing around the NPBEA standards also made the portfolio evaluation more meaningful at a professional level (Wilmore & Erlandson, 1995).

Choosing to adhere to a set of standards is largely a practical matter as opposed a philosophical one. It is unlikely that the public at large has any knowledge of or interest in the alleged absence of professional standards of educational administrators to which the quotation above alludes. Given a choice between enhancing the "professionalization" of educational administration and ensuring that all those who aspire to school leadership dedicate themselves to the success of the students in their care, most would surely choose the latter. Keeping in mind the reality of certification/licensing examinations, however, and the need to establish an organizational framework for the portfolio, consistency with recommended standards is helpful in structuring students' work. The ISLLC standards embody in a broad sense the issues of universal concern across the accrediting agencies. (The full text of the ISLLC standards may be found in appendix A.)

Transforming Pedagogy

Virtually all portfolio models recognize that learning takes place in collaborative circumstances as well as in solitary reflection. It was this element that led to the recognition, noted in the preface, that reforming our assessment process would necessarily entail deeper programmatic changes that were not anticipated at the outset. One of those changes, involving the field dimension of the program, has had an impact on students' preservice experience that has equaled, or perhaps exceeded, the impact of portfolio development itself.

Redistributing the Field Experiences

A central element in the program revision undertaken in 1999 was the redistribution of the required field experiences. Historically, programs in educational administration have relied on a culminating "internship" to provide students with practical experiences in the school environment. Anecdotal evidence suggested, however, that these experiences do not conform to the understanding of the internship as a period of sustained presence in an administrative capacity, an observation that was later confirmed by research conducted by Morgan, Hertzog, and Gibbs (2002) and Hackmann, Schmitt-Oliver, and Tracy (2002). Rather, they tended to consist of a list of discrete tasks the preservice administrator completed in intervals, lending them a kind of transient, fragmentary quality.

The composition of the student body in the field, however, has made any sustained contact between practicing administrators and preservice students difficult at best. Most students pursuing the administrative credential are employed full time elsewhere in the school system, and freeing them from their employment responsibilities for an internship similar to the student teaching experience has thus been impractical if not impossible. Finding the funding to pay for substitute teachers so interns can be relieved of their employment obligations is necessarily problematic.

In the face of that difficulty, most universities have relied on the kind of "interval training" described above. Such an approach has the practical virtue of recognizing the logistical and financial difficulties presented by students' current employment, and thus resolves the dual dilemma of time and money. There are at least two problems, however, with such a model. The first is its reliance on the questionable assumption that students are prepared to engage in those activities only after they have successfully completed all of their coursework. Divorcing the field experience from the epistemological constructs that are meant to ground it makes little sense from an academic perspective. Among the things that prior research had revealed was that students who had completed the program had, in fact, perceived a "gap" of sorts between the coursework, which was to provide a foundation for the experiences, and the experiences themselves (Nicholson & Leary, 2001).

The majority of our students, virtually all of whom are working professionals, attend school part time, and many require up to three years to complete the program. For those, the distance between courses taken early on and the culminating field experience(s) was significant. Although predicated, perhaps, on the penultimate placement of the student teaching experience, such an extrapolation falls victim to an associative fallacy. As an appeal to common practice, it lacks imagination if nothing else.

Second, such a model calls into question the nature of the phenomenon. If, by "internship," we mean the kind of "mind-to-mind contact" described by Geltner (1993), wherein knowledge is "acquired and made meaningful . . . within the actual context of practice," a process that recognizes that students will be completing most of their work outside the school environment (i.e., when they aren't themselves teaching) and relying on hypothetical "in-box" models rather than actual practice bears little resemblance to what is intended: a learning process which is collaborative and which connects "[mentor] and student, learning and action, theory and practice" (p. 5). Students' relationships with their mentors should provide them with the kind of ongoing support and advice that characterized the traditional apprenticeship in which an individual who aspired to become a professional worked under a qualified practitioner and learned through observation and onsite experience.

As Hackmann, Schmitt-Oliver, and Tracy (2002) note, "the ideal clinical experience, for both the organization and the novice, would be a yearlong paid internship" (p. 9). The reason such an opportunity remains the ideal rather than the rule, of course, is that requiring such an experience is simply impossible in most states (North Carolina being one of the notable exceptions). Given the employment status of potential interns, the fiscal issues involved, and the current economic climate in which the federal budget deficit is the highest in the history of the country and educational funding mandates at all levels are increasingly devolving to the states, a yearlong paid internship is likely destined to remain merely an ideal.

In the absence of fully funded yearlong internships, what kind of approach to reducing the distance between preservice programs and the world of practice would sufficiently address the deficiencies of the current model, the divorcing of field experiences from the coursework that is meant to provide their theoretical grounding and the contrived nature of hypothetical exercises? The portfolio assessment approach suggested a possibility.

Central to portfolio models is the understanding that learning takes place in collaborative situations as well as in individual reflection. It is expected that students will develop their portfolios in the company of their colleagues—peers, faculty, and field mentors—discussing folio entries, exploring theoretical underpinnings, and further clarifying their work and philosophies. It was decided, thus, that as the first step in traversing the divide between academic preparation and the world of practice, students would establish relationships with field mentors beginning in the initial course in the program. These relationships, it was hoped, would provide students with the kind of ongoing support and advice that characterized the traditional apprenticeship, and would allow for the practical implementation of concepts being currently examined in their coursework.

The 32 field-based experiences required by the program were subsequently redistributed throughout the curriculum so that each is conducted in conjunction with the course in which the foundational elements inhere. Completing all the field experiences within the span of a single semester, as was the requirement in the previous program, generally meant that students had to enroll for their "internships" during the summer term, when most K–12 schools were not in session. The change was predicated on the premise that even students who are working full time can likely manage to work into their schedules the time necessary to complete a reduced number of experiences in a given semester, particularly if creative use is made of spaces in academic calendars (e.g., days designated as "in-service," periods when students are not in attendance, opportunities provided by year-round schools, and so forth).

This infusion of clinical experiences throughout the program is consistent with calls for "learning opportunities that integrate classroom theory with real-world application" (Hackmann, Schmitt-Oliver, &

Tracy, 2002, p. 2) and for the kinds of "high quality experiences" recommended by Hackmann and English (2001). The activities are neither "trivial" nor "clerical" in nature, nor do they allow for the passive accumulation of hours that concerned Hart and Pounder (1999). Additionally, because the field experiences are conducted in conjunction with students' coursework, they contribute to the enrichment and relevance of classroom discussion envisioned by Cordeiro and Smith-Sloan (1995) and allow for the sharing of problems in a safe environment. A complete list of required field experiences and the courses in which they are embedded can be found in appendix B.

Students also prepare, as part of each field experience, a reflective analysis that examines its epistemological elements. Consistent with the portfolio's emphasis on constructivist learning, the reflective process asks students to examine their experiences to see how they have contributed to their understanding of the dimensions of administrative practice; to interrogate the experiences themselves in an attempt to comprehend their effects, and whether they are reinforced or have reformed students' prior thinking.

Students review the reflective analyses with their mentors prior to committing them to their field folios. This collaborative exploration of how they know what they have come to know about the experience in question and the conscious critiquing of that experience in the interest of discerning its various dimensions has a dual purpose. It is designed to both enhance students' awareness of the importance of examining the connections between what they think and what they do (i.e., supporting our interest in encouraging a reflective practice) and to deepen the relationship between student and mentor. The reactions of both students and mentors, collected since the process was implemented in 1999, have been positive and will be examined in more detail in the epilogue.

Pedagogical Effects

The portfolio process itself is characterized by a series of discussions between the students and their mentors, as well as with peers and faculty, over a period of time, during which both their work and the university's assumptions are open to scrutiny and interrogation. The conversations are likely to center on the field experiences and pedagogical assumptions, for example, on how a particular assignment did or did not prove valuable; on why something succeeded or failed, and what was learned from the experience; on what students needed to know, but did not. Because the self-assessment character of the portfolio is process oriented, students need not wait until they have reached the end of their programs to discover that experiences the university thought valuable proved less than useful, or that some that might have proved useful were overlooked. Students' discussions with mentors can illuminate their preparation in a way that university-based faculty bound by their on-campus commitments cannot.

If we understand pedagogy not as the art or science of teaching, but as the discursive space wherein teaching and learning inform each other, the power of the portfolio process to radically reform pedagogy emerges. Surely part of the art of good teaching is discerning what needs to be taught. Understanding the portfolio as the catalyst for a public debate about what constitutes good practice gives it significant potential to alter not only what and how students learn, but how their learning can help shape our teaching. The isolation of the former professor–student arrangement is replaced by a collaborative assessment involving students, mentors, and university faculty, allowing all involved to reflect on their experiences, question their practices, attempt to comprehend their effects, and either reinforce or reform them. Although the organic nature of this kind of process may prove unsettling to some, it is the only way to get a meaningful answer to the question of knowledge utilization.

Whatever the breadth or depth of a given knowledge base, it is likely insufficient to capture the instrumental problems that await administrative practitioners in the field. Providing students multiple opportunities to actualize their knowledge in the field as they acquire it and to reflect on those experiences can serve not only the constructivist objective, but can reduce the discrepancies between the university's understandings and students' needs. If the ultimate result is a closing of the space between the university and field dimensions of the profession, the complications of living with an organic system will be vindicated.

CHAPTER 4

Implementation Challenges

In a discussion of why so many among the plethora of reforms of the 1980s failed, Fullan (1991) points out that "[t]he tendency [was] widespread for problem solvers to jump from their private plans to public implementation . . . without going through the number of realities necessary to fashion them in accordance with the problems felt by the adult humans whose energy and intelligence [were] needed to implement the plans" (p. 96). It would seem self-evident that not only the consent but the active involvement of those who are needed to effect a successful change must be sought, but the obvious sometimes eludes us in the reform environment where either external pressures can lead us to act in haste or internal dissent can lead us to withdraw from the process.

Vroom's (1964) "valence theory" has some relevance here, with its observation that people who attach high valence or value to a project will find more reasons to be involved in its development and implementation than will those who do not. The first step, as Yvonna Lincoln (as cited in Ryan, 1998) notes, is identifying the stakeholders and convincing them that they have more to gain by participating than by not participating. It is the latter that is potentially problematic. By and large, however, faculty are receptive to what they can perceive as genuinely useful changes in pedagogy, and graduate students are astute enough to distinguish between cosmetic reforms and those that have the potential to enrich their academic experience. The program that is making the transition from conventional to alternative assessment for sound academic reasons should encounter little resistance.

It is in the implementation of radical change that the larger challenges exist. What challenges lie in the development of a project grounded in constructivist principles that conceives of reflection as essential to the student's ability to continue to evolve as a self-directing, inquiring learner, and that essentially shifts the locus for assessment from professor to student? Clearly such an ambitious undertaking will involve both creativity and diligence on the part of all involved, both faculty and students. The transition from an incremental program, wherein students move in a linear fashion through a prescribed sequence of courses, an internship, and a final examination, to one that is more holistic in nature, combining coursework with field-based experiences and relying on self-assessment, is not a simple one.

For faculty, issues of epistemological appropriateness, theoretical underpinnings, and assessment validity are among the matters of concern. Possessing the skills necessary to work in an electronic environment may constitute a complication as well. Students faced with the task of creating an instrument through which they themselves must choose how to demonstrate their capabilities will experience some uncertainty as well, and many might share the same technological anxieties as their professors. Although full consideration of these and other questions is beyond the scope of this text and must be handled in a more immediate context, it is possible to examine some of the initial matters that must be addressed if this kind of multidimensional transformation is to succeed.

FACULTY DIMENSIONS

In her introduction to an account of the Bank Street College of Education's use of portfolio assessment in the teacher education program, Freidus (1998) quotes a student who is struggling to adjust to the learner-centered curriculum: "[This is] an exhausting and yet exhilarating effort. It means, on my part, a long-term commitment to reworking me" (p. 51). Much the same can be said for faculty who decide to undertake the transition from a program that has historically relied on conventional assessment methods. Learning to engage in a curriculum in which assessment relies not on external but internal validation (i.e., not professor- or knowledge-centered but student-centered) requires more than learning new evaluative techniques. Were that the case, making the transition would be a simple matter of learning to substitute one measurement for another. As Freidus notes, however, more is involved than the learning of new practices. "Learning to engage in learner-centered practice, . . . to a great degree, involves unlearning . . . re-imagining the relationship between authority and education" (p. 5).

The unlearning of teaching and assessment practices that have been the foundation of one's practice for years or even decades is no small task. As Freidus's student understands, it entails a "long-term commitment to reworking" oneself. It is a commitment the implications of which should be neither underestimated nor underappreciated. Change is, of course, difficult. Were it not, there would not be hundreds of books providing advice on how to accomplish it. We would be wrong, however, to presume that resistance to a reform of this breadth and depth is simply aversion to change.

Those who perceive the multidimensional nature of this kind of transformation will have genuine concerns, many of which may not emerge at the outset. It is imperative that the program that requires portfolios of its students allow ample time for its faculty to fully address all of the ramifications. Substantive change occurs, as Greene (1994) argues, only over time through a process of construction that is both experiential and dialogical. That process can be rewarding in many ways.

There can be, as Freidus's student suggests, an element of exhilaration that inheres in reworking oneself—a kind of professional renewal, the opportunity for which arises all too rarely in institutions where reforms are more often imposed than elected. Perhaps more valuable than the potential for renewal, however, is the opportunity for faculty to experience for themselves, in a conscious and collaborative way, the complexity of the constructivist process that will ground students' portfolios.

There are, of course, more pragmatic issues with which to contend as well. Faculty will want to ensure that any changes in the assessment approach remain consistent with the institution's mission, and even more important, with the program's or department's objectives. The development of assessment rubrics can be a particularly vexing problem, as interrater reliability tends to rear its head at this juncture, as does the deeply ingrained impulse to standardize any such instrument in the interest of validity. To further complicate the matter, rubrics are preordinate (i.e., they must make clear to students what the requirements for an acceptable portfolio are prior to its construction and presentation). One faculty member characterized it as "trying to develop a scorecard without ever seeing the sport."

All of these concerns will need to be addressed before the details of the portfolio project itself can be implemented, but they need not be resolved completely before conceptualizing the process. In many instances, the development of the project's details will expose some of the broader institutional and programmatic questions, so the process isn't necessarily a linear one. Keeping that in mind is helpful to the developer, as is assuring faculty that both the development and implementation stages are largely organic ones. The process, if conceived from the outset as a fluid one, is simpler to direct from such a perspective.

STUDENT DIMENSIONS

Students, too, may be required to "unlearn" some things, among them the conventional assessment model that places the faculty at the center of the process. What structure might offer a suitable framework for a project that places students at the center of their own assessment? It has been established that the development of a portfolio allows students to integrate their academic preparation with their experiential education by asking them to consciously relate the two. It is also helpful, however, to adopt MacIsaac's (1991) distinction between the *portfolio* and the *folio*. The portfolio contains only those entries chosen by the developer to demonstrate proficiency or comprehension of a specific set of skills or body of knowledge, and to address in a conscious way his or her professional growth and development. The folio is less discriminatory, including the accumulated body of work for a course, project, or program.

In other words, as Barrett (1995) describes the distinction, a folio represents the total population of evidence documenting the student's learning experience, while the portfolio can be seen as a select sample of the total population (p. 200). The predominant feature of the folio is its breadth, while the portfolio is best characterized by its depth. The complete intellectual product students develop for the preservice principals' portfolio will include both. Before describing each element, however, a word about how students' work is documented is necessary. If the project is to be seen as holistic, it is important that students have an integrated environment in which to work.

Documenting Progress

Students constructing a preservice portfolio will receive a dual evaluation of both the folios and the portfolio, as the work serves both the institutional requirement for grades for the respective courses and the requirement for portfolio completion. Although these are certainly not mutually exclusive, it may be helpful to conceive of the grade as the quantitative assessment and the folio–portfolio evaluation as the qualitative assessment. The latter will follow the guidelines detailed in the assessment rubrics, which in their current iteration can be seen in appendices C, D, and E, and are further discussed in the epilogue.

Rubrics and other relevant materials are under constant review and are updated for students and faculty on the university's leadership portfolio website. Because of the organic nature of the portfolio process, and because our migration to an online course delivery system means that much of the interaction students have with one another and with faculty is conducted via the Internet, we thought it necessary to provide a place for them to remain in contact with both the project and the people involved. (One student described it as "portfolio homeroom.")

The website not only provides information concerning portfolio construction and assessment, but gives students access to a records page where they can keep track of their progress through the program. Assessments for each of their folios are entered on the website, and all folio columns must show completion of the respective requirements before students can enroll in the capstone course. A bulletin board function offers a forum for public discussions or questions, a chat function allows students to engage in "real-time" conversations with faculty or other students, and a private e-mail option allows for contact between and among faculty and students on issues that are inappropriate for public discussion.

Students are entered into the website database when they enroll in the introductory course and remain there until their graduation. Those who have completed the program confirmed that it was an invaluable resource for them, particularly in terms of the sense of community it provides. They also appreciated both the practical aspect of having access to an aggregate assessment of their work and the personal satisfaction of being able to visibly chart their progress.

The Course Folio

Because licensure/certification requirements stipulate that students submit to a formal assessment to affirm their acquisition of certain cognitive skills and demonstrate the capacity for applying them, the portfolio project is comprised in part of 12 individual folios, each representing students' academic work in the courses required for completing the degree. Each course folio provides evidence of how the student met the requirements for the course, as determined by the professor and congruent with the Leadership Studies Program Principles and the ISLLC *Standards for School Leaders* (1996). The professor of record evaluates each student's course folio and designates the folio as exceptional, acceptable, or unacceptable. Unacceptable folios must be revised to the satisfaction of the professor of record before the capstone project may be undertaken.

The Field Experience Folio

Because each course in the program requires an associated field experience or experiences, students' accounts of their field experiences will likely reside in their respective course folios. In the interest of expediting the assessment process, however, particularly in light of the requirements of accreditation agencies, students will include on their disks and websites (if they choose to develop them) a separate folio for the field experiences associated with their coursework. Creation of this folio involves two steps.

The first is the simple copying of the field experience file from the associated course folio. The second is the inclusion of a narrative piece that reflects on the nature of the field experience, its relative-value, difficulties in implementation or interpretation, and so forth. Both the professors-of-record and field mentors will review the field experience folios with students, with the respective professors entering the designations of exceptional, acceptable, or unacceptable. This clustering of files alleviates evaluators' searching through individual course folios to locate specific information related to field experiences.

The Reflection Folio

Programs designed to help students become critically reflective practitioners value reflection for its contribution to both individual growth and collaborative practice. A sense of purpose, in individuals and groups, serves as an orienting principle in uncertain or difficult circumstances, and that sense of purpose is derived from cultivating a habit for reflection. Effective leaders are those who understand how their thoughts and actions shape their reality and who consistently examine themselves in those terms. We have not historically asked students in educational administration programs to engage in this kind of thinking, choosing instead to focus on the structural dimensions of the field.

Peter Senge is among the business leaders who question the conflation of corporate management and leadership. In *The Fifth Discipline* (1990), he argues that corporate management theory, which embodies the Ramistic principle of breaking apart problems or processes to make them more manageable, extracts a "hidden, enormous price":

> We can no longer see the consequences of our actions; we lose our intrinsic sense of connection to a larger whole. When we then try to see 'the big picture,' . . . to reassemble the fragments in our minds . . . the task is futile. (p. 3)

That futility is born not of incompetence, but of inexperience. It is no surprise that graduates whose only exposure to the classical liberal arts curriculum was the "general studies" courses required of them as freshmen and sophomores in undergraduate school fail to demonstrate proficiency in holistic thinking. In the gradual professionalization of higher education, the interdisciplinarity that inheres in the traditional liberal arts curriculum was lost as students, and the job market, showed an increasing interest in specialization. Paradoxically enough, it may be that same job market that restores a more reflective approach to leadership education.

Although liberal arts study is deeply rooted in the classical tradition, it remains the contemporary engine of practical reason in human affairs. It is instructive to keep in mind that the word "liberal" in the phrase "liberal arts" comes not from the Latin *liber* meaning book, but from the other Latin *liber,* meaning free. The whole point of liberal arts study is to liberate its students; to expose them to a multiplicity of perspectives across a range of academic subjects that will allow them to enlarge the boundaries of their personal worlds. Max DePree (1989) recognizes this quality in *Leadership Is an Art*: "This book is about the art of leadership: liberating people to do what is required of them in the most effective and humane way possible" (p. 1). Peter Drucker (1989) agrees with that assessment in his description of management as a liberal art:

> [M]anagers draw on all the knowledges and insights of the humanities and the social sciences—on psychology and philosophy, on economics and history, on the physical sciences and ethics. . . . For these reasons, management will increasingly be the discipline and the practice through which the "humanities" will again acquire recognition, impact and relevance. (p. 231)

Until Peter Ramus pillaged the rhetorical canon, separating philosophy from rhetoric, and thus thought from action, helping students understand the practical connection between the two was precisely what the academy did. By asking students to develop a disposition for reflection, to internalize the process, development of the portfolio can create an ongoing opportunity for them to sustain the practice and help to restore that connection. A significant aspect of the portfolio process, thus, is a folio devoted to students' reflections concerning the practice of educational leadership. This reflection folio will constitute a third folder in their projects and will include six essays in which they explore the practical ramifications of the principles that provide the foundation for their programs of study.

The principles of Marshall University's leadership studies program are, as are the corresponding ISLLC standards, grounded in a normative assumption (i.e., that these are principles/standards that are fundamental to or "normal" in the practice of educational leadership). Therefore, an exploration of the value of collaboration, for example, or the benefits of lifelong learning would constitute an exercise in tautology that would be of little benefit to students. The purpose of the reflection folio is to give students a space in which to think about the potential difficulties that inhere in implementing certain theoretical constructs in practice. As is the case with the field experience folios, students discuss the entries in their reflection folios with both their mentors and members of the faculty. The latter will enter the designation of exceptional, acceptable, or unacceptable into the student database. Unacceptable entries must be revised to the satisfaction of the evaluating professor.

Included on the homepage for the preservice portfolio are suggestions to assist the student in the preparation of each of the reflective essays required, exploring each of the principles/standards, their underlying pretexts, and some related questions. The student's approach to discussing them, of course, will not be limited to the suggestions provided therein. The questions are offered only to illustrate some reflective possibilities, and these writing prompts may be found in appendix F.

Rather than arbitrarily connect these essays to a particular course, students are advised to write them independently at the time they feel they are prepared to address them. A suggested timeline for submission of the reflective essays, however, is on the homepage as well. Students are encouraged to approach the reflection folio on their own terms in the hope that its creation helps not only to engender that understanding, but to contribute by extension to their practice.

The Ethics Folio

Schools, like other institutions, both reflect and project the broader culture. The same tensions that plague us in the outside world are played out inside the school—tensions grounded in the difficulties of dealing with difference, of learning how to balance competing needs and interests—and what students learn while they are there determines what they carry with them into the world when they leave. It is imperative that they have leaders who can demonstrate an understanding of what Sirotnik (1990) calls "moral ecology," a recognition of "the delicate balance of moral relationships" (p. 321).

There is some debate, within the educational leadership discipline, concerning whether ethics should be taught as a separate course or whether ethical considerations are best examined in connection with issues that surface throughout the curriculum. Our decision conforms to the latter position. If students are to see ethical reasoning as an integral element of their eventual leadership practice, acquiring it as a habit of mind is imperative. For that reason, we think it important enough to infuse it throughout the program of study.

An ethical reasoning model (developed from Herlong, 1985, and Holifield and Dickinson, 2001), explicating five approaches to the resolution of moral problems, is provided in the required introductory course in the principalship program. Students are asked to apply various components of the model in problem-based assignments in each course as they progress toward the completion of their degrees. As is the case with the course folios, the professor of record evaluates the students' work since the assignments are part of the respective courses. There is no separate assessment entered in the portfolio website, and there is no specific assessment rubric for these assignments. Maintaining their work in the ethics folio, however, ensures they will be able to access it readily as they assemble their portfolios in the capstone course.

The Ancillary Folio

As was observed in chapter 1, educators are well aware that professional growth occurs in circumstances other than those related solely to students' academic programs. The development of the portfolio, thus, also provides a place for students to gather evidence of their learning in other environments. Participation in or presentations made to conventions or annual meetings of professional organizations, faculty or staff development workshops, grant-writing experiences, presentations to policymaking bodies, committee work, participation in civic organizations, parent–teacher conferences, and preparation of articles for publication all constitute potentially valuable experiences students may wish to document. They may wish to keep track as well of performance evaluations, any honors, awards, or commendations, and an updated version of their résumés. Although this folio will not be subject to assessment as are the others, including it on the portfolio disk or website offers an opportunity for students to both supplement academic work and demonstrate proficiencies that add an element of diversity to their work.

THE PORTFOLIO

As was noted earlier, we have chosen to adopt MacIsaac's (1991) distinction between the folio and the portfolio in order to clarify the final step in the students' projects. The folios detailed above represent the accumulated body of evidence documenting students' learning processes, the predominant feature of which is breadth. The culminating entry, characterized by its depth, is the portfolio. Its construction constitutes a more discriminatory act, one that Schulman (1998) describes as theoretical:

> [Assembling a] portfolio is a theoretical act. By that I mean that every time you design, organize, or create in your education program a template, a framework, or a model for a . . . portfolio, you are engaged in an act of theory. . . . What is declared worth documenting, worth reflecting on, what is deemed to be portfolio-worthy is a theoretical act. (p. 24)

In the same way that teaching, for Schulman and others, is conceived not as a skilled behavior but as "a form of thought and judgment" (p. 24), the conception of leadership in Marshall's leadership studies program is one that focuses not on the mastery of behavioral techniques but on the development of intellectual and personal qualities that will allow administrators to shape and reshape their practices over the course of their professional lives. It is an understanding that challenges the notion that the study of leadership can be approached generically by taking the position that its practice is, in fact, extraordinarily personalized, conditioned by the unique insights and capabilities of those who aspire to it.

Such an understanding requires an assessment approach that allows students to reflect on and to demonstrate those qualities in a way that is meaningful for them. The construction of the portfolio, assembled during the capstone course, is thus a two-step process. The first step is the choosing of which artifacts to include (i.e., the identification of those items that make explicit the theoretical foundations of conceptions of leadership). It is a process that, as Clarke's (1995) research indicates, is directly in the service of making conscious one's leadership philosophy. Lyons's (1998) experience with students who have constructed teaching portfolios, however, has made clear that the act of selecting artifacts representative of their philosophies is insufficient to imbue the process with meaning: "[T]he portfolio development process alone does not reveal the process of meaning making. . . . Only in reflecting on 'why' may a person's own interpretation of meaning be made evident" (p. 116).

The second step, then, grounded in the work of Vygotsky (1978) and Bruner (1986), who argue that we come to know ourselves primarily through our interactions with others, is a public seminar where students present the completed portfolio. The setting is designed to engage students, faculty, peers, and field mentors in a collaborative inquiry that ultimately invites all participants to revisit their own leadership philosophies, the goal of which is to internalize the explaining, elaborating, and interrogating of our respective understandings in a learning community as an ongoing element of professional practice.

The portfolio is at the center of an assessment model predicated on self-designed inquiry and realized through clarification and justification. At its center is the transformation of leadership from technical skill to theoretical act, undertaken and sustained by the student. It is the student who will enable that transformation, who will look critically at him- or herself and his or her work, and who will act on that critique to improve his or her practice. Such reflection, as Bolin (1988) notes, is not a given of the human condition. It should be. The goal of the portfolio is to create an opportunity for its internalization.

CHAPTER 5

Portfolio Design Issues

For the faculty who find the research on constructivist learning and the value of reflection persuasive and who have decided to reform their evaluation practices in order to provide students the maximum opportunity to learn and demonstrate the process of self-assessment, the implementation of a portfolio requirement is a logical one. The obvious next issue is the shape it will take, literally. Will it be a conventional three-ring binder with multiple narratives but little else? Will videotapes and audiotapes be permitted to supplement the notebook? What other artifacts might be anticipated? Beyond the obvious practical problems of maintaining the more conventional portfolio (e.g., storage space, the inherent difficulties of preserving paper, photographs, and tapes), there is the deeper epistemological matter of consistency of process and product.

The choice of an electronic format for the preservice principal portfolio has a dual rationale. As was discussed in chapter 3 on conceptual development, the *process* of portfolio development is grounded in constructivist principles, the primary component of which is that one learns by actively constructing what he or she needs to know. The development of the portfolio in a technological environment, wherein students have available the means to both conceptually connect the links between and among their learning experiences and illustrate them visually, constitutes precisely the kind of experience that can provide a constructivist foundation for their lifelong learning. If, as Quintilian argued, the purpose of an education is to give one the tools to participate more fully in life, and if we are honest about what that means, we will concede that we don't always know what the necessary tools are. What we do know is that no one has all the answers; that we are frequently in situations that require us to say "I don't know." Given how quickly things change, however, not knowing is not a failure; it is a common condition.

Consider the contemporary workplace. By the time we fully understand a process or procedure, the circumstances under which we learned it have probably changed. It can be an incredibly frustrating situation if we aren't prepared for it. Unless we understand and help our students understand the value of *constructing* knowledge as opposed to *receiving* it, we will not only have failed Quintilian, we will have failed our students and ourselves. If one of the things we expect of ourselves in educational administration is that we can develop an architectonic approach to leadership that conceives of critical thinking as making meaningful connections, capitalizing on available technologies to develop that ability is a valuable learning experience.

From the *product* perspective, constructing the portfolio in an electronic environment has a number of advantages as well. The digital format allows for portability and ease of handling (for both students' purposes and university files); expedites editing; provides options that are either unavailable or awkwardly achieved in conventional portfolios (e.g., qualitative research can capitalize on video streaming, audio recording, and scanning documents as opposed to submitting reams of paper and video- and cassette tapes); includes a broad range of statistical packages for documenting research; simplifies backup; and represents an easily accessible credential for potential employers as it can be loaded to a website, copied to a Zip disk, or burned on a compact disc. Additionally, as emerging technologies expand the dimensions of the classroom, demands are made on education professionals to comprehend not only their potential but their application as well. Principals who have demonstrated technological proficiency through the construction of an electronic product will be saved the embarrassing double standard of exhorting faculty to integrate technology into their teaching while steadfastly avoiding its use themselves.

MEDIA CHOICES

One of the advantages of developing the portfolio in an electronic format is that it allows students the option to choose among several storage and construction alternatives. As a general rule, students select media programs and formats with which they are comfortable, since the point, after all, is to focus on the epistemological issues as opposed to the electronic. The central question remains *How do you know what you know?* not *How accomplished are you with technology?* The development and presentation of the portfolio in the electronic environment is a means to an end, not an end in itself; thus, it is important to maintain the focus on the assessment rationale for the process. Still, to the extent that the portfolio and/or presentation can be enhanced by the creative use of multimedia, students are encouraged to explore the range of options available and to take advantage of the university's resources.

STORAGE: WEB PAGE OR DISK?

Advantages of the Web Page

Storing the information on the World Wide Web can be a dynamic and cost-effective way to create and maintain the portfolio, allowing students to access and edit their work from virtually anywhere via an Internet connection. They can also share their work without the cost of copying and providing disks (and incurring postage costs, when necessary), and there is no special software required for audiences to view the portfolio.

One benefit of storing the work on a web page is that the student isn't burdened by keeping track of disks. Disks are easy to misplace or damage and, without a backup, months of work can be lost instantly. Placing the portfolio on a web page also provides a constant point of access, despite the occasional instability of the Internet. There may be times when outages make connections problematic, but once service is restored, the material will be there. In most cases, the system administrator does daily backups of the server on which the student's work is stored; thus, if for some reason the server is permanently disabled, the administrator can restore the files to a new server.

The wide range of skill levels accomodated by web page design packages makes this option increasingly appealing for students. Using a variety of editing tools, students can be beginning users and still create attractive pages. From the basic text editors packaged with the operating systems on computers to fairly sophisticated web page editing software programs, students have numerous choices available to them for designing creative pages.

Disadvantages of the Web Page

Among the drawbacks with web pages is available bandwidth. If students have prepared web pages that are high in graphic content or use video or audio, they, and potential evaluators, may find themselves waiting a long time for the information to download. If a portfolio featuring significant levels of video, audio, or images is planned, for example, a page on the World Wide Web may not be the best choice.

In addition to the technical issues, students will want to consider the matter of web security. How secure do they want their documents to be? Is it acceptable for the world at large to view their work? Their personal information? Those kinds of questions are inevitable when information is stored on the web. Pages can be password-protected, but such a process requires a level of skill that often eludes many, and even with password-protection, security cannot be guaranteed. Efficient hackers have broken into everything from local websites to U.S. government pages.

Students may also want to think about how they intend to use their web pages subsequent to the presentation in the capstone course. If viewing the portfolio is essential to an interview, for example, difficulties can arise. As was noted above, the web is not completely stable, and not everyone or every office has an on-demand Internet connection. Students who choose the web for storing their portfolios will want backup copies of their sites, either on a Zip disk or a CD-ROM, in case the Internet connection is unavailable or slow at a critical time. Students should also bear in mind that possible concerns over security or even server space could result in their having to move their web pages to another location, which will be problematic if the URL has already been provided to a potential employer.

Finally, the circumstances for the capstone presentation itself must be considered. If the computer provided for the demonstration cannot be connected to the Internet, students will have no choice but to resort to several floppy disks, a Zip disk, or a CD-ROM. Although it is unlikely that universities lack multiple media options, it is always a possibility that some of them won't be available on the day or in the room scheduled for the symposium. It is also possible that the Zip drive, for example, will handle 100 MB disks, but not 250s, or that the audio or video formats students have used will be incompatible with equipment provided for the presentation. Students will need to work closely during the capstone course with faculty and media services staff to ensure that the full range of their multimedia presentations can be demonstrated.

SOFTWARE CHOICES

In addition to determining the best choice for storing the portfolio, students will need to identify the software environment in which they feel most comfortable. Bearing in mind the fact that constructing the portfolio in an electronic environment is not an end in itself, the skill level of the student is nonetheless important if the process of preparing the finished product is not to turn into an exercise in technological frustration that overwhelms its academic value. Factors such as adeptness at using a computer in general must be taken into account. Is the student usually the individual asking all the questions or the one who is answering them? Those who are novices may need to take the simpler route for composing the portfolio, starting, for example, with a program like Microsoft's PowerPoint and then moving on to more sophisticated design software if they wish.

Time and motivation are also critical. How much time, realistically, does the student have to devote to the construction of the portfolio? Does he or she work full time? Are there family responsibilities? Other professional development commitments that have to be met? If finding additional time is a factor, a program like PowerPoint will likely be the fastest as well as the easiest. In terms of personal satisfaction, will meeting the minimal requirements be sufficient to the student, or does he or she want to raise the bar, so to speak, for those who follow? If that is the case, more advanced authoring software will allow the kinds of creative touches that lead to a more sophisticated presentation.

In addition to ease of use, access to software and equipment are obvious considerations as well. It stands to reason that students will likely work with what is most accessible to them, either at home or on the job—particularly if they are part-time students and cannot get to campus on a regular basis. Most universities, however, have available and will permit student use of various media (e.g., scanners, video or audio capturing devices, recordable CD drives, and so forth) for creating the files students wish to incorporate into their presentations. A close working relationship between the computer services unit and the program unit can ensure that the former understands the dimensions of the project and the latter can recommend students to them for assistance.

Text Editors and Web Page Design Packages

As was noted above, there is a wide range of web page design packages covering most skill levels that makes this option attractive to students. They may choose the basic text editors that come with the operating systems on PCs, some of which provide formatting options in HTML (hypertext markup language) to prepare files for the Internet, or use specialized web page editing packages. Using a text editor like WordPerfect or Microsoft Word sometimes requires more specialized knowledge, however, than does a web page editing package (e.g., FrontPage or Netscape Composer), depending upon the version available. More recent versions of the former, however, are increasing in "user friendliness." Additional software is sometimes needed to upload the pages prepared with a text editor to a website, which is often included with the operating system or can be downloaded free of charge through the Internet. Web page editors, on the other hand, require minimal knowledge of web page programming. A range of options is available between the basic text editor and the web page editing software, among them the editor that comes with the Netscape Internet browser. Netscape's built-in Composer program allows authors to create web pages that are elementary to intermediate in sophistication in a WYSIWYG (what you see is what you get) environment.

PowerPoint

Among the programs our students have found both user-friendly and visually attractive is Microsoft's PowerPoint. Even computer novices can quickly create professional-looking interactive presentations, incorporating graphics, audio, video, animations, and hyperlinks in a creative multimedia demonstration. They need not be design experts to construct effective presentations since PowerPoint includes a broad range of templates, and as their proficiency with the program increases, students will be able to add more customized components to their files. PowerPoint comes as a standard component of the Microsoft Office package, so many individuals and companies already have it on their own computers, making both creation and viewing relatively simple.

A common problem students encounter with PowerPoint is that the ease with which graphics can be incorporated leads to files of significant size. It isn't at all difficult to exhaust available space on a floppy disk with only a handful of PowerPoint slides if those slides include substantial amounts of video or animation, so students who don't wish to have to manage multiple floppies will want to copy the presentation to storage medium with more capacity. If they lack the equipment to do that, they can store the presentation on a series of floppy disks and then bring those to the computer lab to be copied to a single Zip disk or burned onto a CD.

One built-in feature of PowerPoint is the option to save files in HTML, which allows students to save their portfolios as web pages if they wish to upload them to the Internet at a later time. It is possible, however, that when files are saved in HTML, animations and some internal links may be lost.

There are, of course, alternatives to creating the portfolios other than those mentioned herein, and their number can only be expected to increase. Some will be even more "user friendly" than those currently available, some more challenging, and they will run the gamut of expense and learning curve. The crucial point to keep in mind is that the portfolio is meant to be viewed, and that others who need to view the product or with whom students wish to share it may not have access to the newest or most sophisticated computer software or hardware. Although it may be tempting to indulge in the latest technology, giving in may result in a portfolio that can be accessed in only the most high-tech environments. If the symposium audience or a potential employer can see only part of the presentation, it will have lost its impact.

PUTTING IT TOGETHER

Before construction of the portfolio begins, it may be helpful to follow a technique referred to as storyboarding, which focuses on the selection of information the student wants to see on each page. It isn't a complex technological undertaking, and can be as easily done on a sheet of paper as on a computer. To an extent, elements of the presentation have been predetermined through the guidelines for the project disseminated in the capstone course (e.g., framing statements, identification of themes, required artifacts), and the relevant content issues will be examined in the next chapter. Here, I present primarily the technological issues.

Among the issues to be considered are page layout, visibility of the theme, navigation concerns, contrast, font styles, consistency, images and sound effects, and copyright laws.

- In terms of *page layout*, the primary concern is balance. Does the page look as if one side is congested while the other is empty? Is there too much information for the space available? Is there sufficient blank space so the elements aren't crowded?
- The *thematic framework* needs to be readily discernible. If someone were to leave the presentation and reenter five pages/slides later, could he tell from the consistency of the format that he is watching the same presentation? Would he know which element/standard is being discussed?
- The presentation should be easy for those viewing it alone to follow, so *navigational tools* are essential. An excessive number of links from a single page can be wearisome to viewers, who generally dislike wading through a long series of pages to arrive at the piece of information they are seeking. The rule of thumb is to use no more than four links in succession. Additionally, whether it is a website or PowerPoint presentation, viewers typically need to be able to find their way back to the main or primary menu page, so including a button or link in the same place on each page is advisable. If links are provided, it is critical to ensure they are functional. When links are added, a promise is made to the viewer, and breaking that promise suggests either poor organization or failure

to properly maintain the portfolio. Neither is impressive to a viewer. Monitoring the links for currency is essential.

- For obvious reasons, *contrast* is crucial. Light text on a white background virtually ensures that few viewers will have the patience to read what is there. The same is true for dark text on a dark background, and in some cases for fluorescent text on any background. Although there are alternatives to standard black text on a white background, students will want to be certain that the content isn't sacrificed for color. If multiple color schemes are preferred, web design experts recommend that there be no more than three or four per page (i.e., a background, a primary text color, and one or two others for emphasis, if necessary).
- Like contrast, choosing an appropriate *font* can mean the difference between a portfolio that is viewed in its entirety and one that is dismissed within minutes. Choosing an artistic font is pointless if viewers find it difficult to decipher. On the other hand, part of the fun of creating an electronic document is the multitude of presentation options available. As a general rule, sans serif (literally "without wings") fonts are preferred for presentations that are to be viewed on a screen, so Arial or Futura could be more easily read than Lucinda Handwriting or Matisse. Novelty fonts can be used, of course, to perhaps call attention to a particularly salient element or for emphasis; but they should be used sparingly. In order to capitalize on creative possibilities without sacrificing readability, it is generally a good idea to view the presentation on more than one computer in order to check page appearance.
- *Consistency* in presentation lends a professional aspect to the portfolio. Changes in background color, borders, navigational buttons, font style, and so forth from page to page can distract from the content of the presentation. The point is to get the viewer to concentrate on the material, not on continuing shifts in appearance.
- The use of *visual or audio effects* can significantly enhance a presentation, provided they have a purpose, aren't distracting, and aren't time-consuming for the viewer. If the use of special effects results in forcing the viewer to wait interminably for them to load, any impact they may have had is likely lost. Links to some websites offering free graphics and sounds are generally provided on

the homepage or in handout material for the capstone course. Some, however, have restrictions (e.g., they may not be permitted for commercial purposes), so students will need to read the use agreements carefully.
- Finally, consideration of *copyright* laws is imperative. If images, sounds, text, or other information from the web or other sources are being used, it is absolutely crucial to know whether the material is protected by a copyright. If it is, appropriate credit must be given to the author. Several websites exist to provide information on copyright issues, and the advice of faculty and computer services staff can be sought as well.

As the assessment rubric for the portfolio shows (appendix E), both the portfolio and its presentation in the capstone symposium can be enhanced by thoughtful selection and innovative use of multimedia options. It is important to note, however, that this element is mentioned but once, and that the bulk of the rubric is given over to such matters as the demonstration of sustained reflection, the cogent expression of ideas, the comprehension of program principles and their relationship to the ISLLC standards and dispositions, the recognition of the interdependence of theory and practice, and the explicit examination of personal and professional growth throughout the student's matriculation.

Having access to all the technological innovations in the universe will not relieve students of the cognitive heavy lifting necessary to address those concerns. The construction of a portfolio is first and foremost an internal process, subsumed entirely in the mind, and the computers on which students work will offer no remedies for a lack of ideas. They can, however, simplify finding some of the information that underlies those ideas, provide ready connections to additional information that either challenges or reinforces those ideas, and allow the student to explicate the connections between and among them in a way that may otherwise be difficult to demonstrate.

Thoreau's (1854) thinking on emerging technologies may help keep the electronic element in perspective. Although perhaps not a complete Luddite, his response to advanced telecommunications was something less than enthusiastic. "Our inventions," he noted, "are wont to be pretty toys, which distract our attention from serious things. They are but improved means to an unimproved end. . . . We are in great haste to construct a magnetic telegraph from Maine to Texas; but Maine and Texas, it may be, have nothing important to communicate." Students who "have nothing important to communicate" will find that even the most sophisticated use of technology will fail to compensate. On the means–end continuum, they are advised to keep the end in sight at all times.

ASSESSMENT CONCERNS

As was noted in chapter 4 on implementation challenges, moving to a curriculum that is learner-centered as opposed to professor-centered represents a significant shift in the academic lives of both students and faculty. The transition, as Freidus (1998) notes, "involves unlearning . . . re-imagining the relationship between authority and education" (p. 5). The difficulties in reimagining the locus of authority become most visible as students set themselves to the task of constructing the portfolio.

Although they have been committing their various assignments, field-work, reflections, and ancillary experiences to their respective folios throughout the program, many students fail to think about the actual integration of the folios into the portfolio until they reach the capstone course. What frequently ensues is a period of intense frustration born of years of having been told precisely what to do in order to demonstrate their acquisition of certain skills and/or content. Those who have learned all too well the process of giving to academic authority precisely what it requests, and who have prided themselves on doing so in a commendable fashion, seem cut adrift when confronted with the demand to frame the dimensions of assessment themselves. Not knowing "what faculty want" elicits a deep fear of producing work that might be found less than acceptable (or for those high achievers, less than perfect).

It is equally difficult for faculty members, who too have been acculturated to an academic climate wherein it is they who bear responsibility for developing evaluative measures, to know the extent of their roles in a constructivist undertaking. The development of the portfolio, with its transference of the central assessment role to the student, can leave both parties somewhat uncertain. Students may worry that the final product won't rise to the expectations of the faculty. Faculty may be concerned they aren't providing adequate guidance.

The fact that the terrain appears challenging, however, is insufficient reason for leaving it unexplored. In the same way that rubric design can be undermined by the well-developed habit to standardize in the interest of "fairness" or "objectivity," the composition of the portfolio can be rendered uniform by the imposition of templates or other such structural frameworks. The challenge is to find the balance between providing support and compromising the constructivist process. If we truly want our students to be independent learners, we have to give them the confidence to accept that knowledge can be understood only as it is constructed by them in their own minds and that they have the latitude to demonstrate that knowledge in a manner that best represents them.

CHAPTER 6

Epilogue

As the preservice principal portfolio has been in place for only 12 semesters, any conclusions that could be drawn concerning its success would be more speculative than established. Lyons (1998) notes that there does not yet exist "a body of systematic data documenting [portfolios'] uses or long-term consequences" in teacher education (p. 247). The research base is even thinner as it relates to the effectiveness of portfolio use in educational leadership.

Fifty-one students enrolled in our leadership studies program under the new requirements have presented their completed portfolios in the capstone symposium. The compilation of any substantial data will have to await a longitudinal study that focuses on the actual practices of these 51, and of the more than 200 students who have yet to complete the program. It is possible, however, by reviewing the portfolios themselves, as explored in the capstone presentations, and the students' self- and program evaluations (appendix G), to draw some measures of the impact such a process can have for students. This chapter undertakes that initial review. It will also address some lessons learned by the faculty thus far, and will sketch the dimensions of the planned meta-assessment (i.e., the assessment of the portfolio assessment process).

THE CAPSTONE EXPERIENCE

As was noted in chapter 4 on implementation issues, the final requirement for students in the program is the construction and presentation of the portfolio itself. Because our leadership studies program centers on the value of knowledge utilization, we believe students require an opportunity to demonstrate proficiency in converting propositional knowledge (i.e., content or theory) into procedural knowledge (i.e., practice), and to verify as well their comprehension of program principles and the ISLLC standards (appendix A).

Based on Schulman's (1998) characterization of portfolio design as a theoretical act, the capstone experience also provides an opportunity for both students and faculty to engage in an analysis of their personal and professional growth through a process that requires them to examine their own theoretical orientations (i.e., the assumptions that inform their practice). It is a requirement that reinforces our understanding of leadership as a deeply personalized practice, informed by the individual perspectives and abilities of those who aspire to it.

Students choose the artifacts they will include, selecting those they believe best represent the theoretical foundations of their conceptions of leadership, that illustrate their skill in converting theory into practice, and that confirm their understanding of the program principles and ISLLC standards. Among the requirements are identification of connections between and among those artifacts, the association of a theme with those connections, and the presentation of the completed portfolio in a public symposium that involves students, field mentors, and leadership studies faculty members. The portfolio becomes part of the CD that students submit as a graduation requirement, which also includes their individual course folios, field experience folios, reflection folios, and ancillary and ethics folios.

The symposium is designed to engage students, faculty, peers, and field mentors in a collaborative inquiry into the dimensions of the preservice experience. Are the program principles and accreditation standards sufficient to provide a foundation for beginning an administrative practice? Does the construction of a portfolio representative of coursework, field experiences, and reflective orientations give students adequate opportunity to exemplify that foundation? How do we know when a student has done so? Are the evaluation rubrics for assessing the respective folios and the portfolio valid? Most important, how can preservice programs arrange their requirements so that all students can acquire the desired knowledge, skills, and dispositions?

These questions and others that surfaced during postsymposium debriefing were addressed through a two-phase evaluation. The first involved the gathering of preprogram data from students and their field mentors through an interview protocol that featured an open-ended dialogue wherein they examined together the issue of preservice preparation as it relates to administrative practice. Students conducted the interviews as part of the required field experiences for the introductory course in the program. They examined the themes that emerged, attempting to discern those that made explicit (i.e., specific concerns regarding preservice preparation) what had been largely implicit (i.e., the perception of a theory–practice gap), in an effort to bring focus to their own preparation.

The second phase featured the retrieval of those interviews for purposes of comparing what students' mentors had characterized as deficiencies in their own preservice preparation with the program the students had just completed. The second interview analyses were combined with the collection of additional postprogram data, including the students' self- and program evaluations as well as informal assessments offered by faculty, field mentors, and the students themselves in the debriefing session following the portfolio symposium. Their thinking is summarized below.

The Faculty View

From the faculty perspective, it appears the decision to replace the comprehensive examination with a portfolio-based assessment was a sound one. All full-time faculty members involved in the master's degree program in leadership studies have participated in each symposium, and all have expressed satisfaction with the transition. The consensus is that the processes of self-designed inquiry, clarification, and justification demonstrated in the students' presentations provide both a breadth and depth of information that is difficult if not impossible to discern in data resulting from a standardized licensing test or comprehensive examination. One remarked, tongue in cheek, that he had "no idea we prepared such articulate graduates." The transformation of leadership from technical skill to theoretical act conforms well to our interest in expanding outcomes beyond cognitive capability and to our emphasis on knowledge utilization.

The degree to which graduates find their learning experiences useful in the world of practice is of particular concern to us. Whatever the extent of an administrative "knowledge base," it is likely inadequate to prepare practitioners for the unpredictability of their work. Providing students multiple opportunities to actualize their knowledge in the field as they acquire it and to subsequently reflect on those experiences in a formal and public fashion can serve not only the constructivist objective, but can reduce the discrepancies between the university's understandings and students' needs. One faculty member addressed this potentiality:

> I know we try to stay on top of what goes on in schools; but the fact is we're pretty much confined to campus. Most of our understanding is anecdotal. We hear what students tell us about their work environments, we read the papers, we track educational policy. But we aren't *there* on a daily basis.

Another commented on the value of having the field mentors participate in the symposium in terms of how it can contribute to faculty's understanding of schools' needs:

> I can't emphasize enough how critical it is for us to maintain an open dialogue with practicing principals. Students keep us informed about changes in policies and procedures, but it's from a teacher's perspective. To really get a handle on how those things affect school leadership, we have to have contact with those who have that responsibility.

This is especially critical as it relates to our obligation to students, but is important to us as well in connection to projected shortages in the numbers of principals willing to take on the job of leading schools. That subject was the focus of many of the mentors' observations.

The Mentors' Responses

The field mentors who have been able to attend the portfolio symposia and subsequent debriefing share a common concern: the thinning of their ranks with projected retirements and the widely publicized scarcity of candidates to replace those who leave the profession. They are familiar with reports such as that issued by Blackman and Fenwick (2000), which identifies the average age of practicing principals as nearly 50 and projects that nearly 40% of the nation's 93,200 current principals are ready to retire. Using the U.S. Department of Labor statistics, they estimate the need for school administrators to increase by a minimum of 10 to 20% through 2005.

Mentors are also aware that those figures reflect not a dearth of certified professionals to assume positions of school leadership, but a host of conditions that make the position unattractive to those who are eligible to fill it. They see as the key solution more realistic training and meaningful professional development at the preservice phase, and all of those involved with the first 51 students to complete the revised program see it as a dramatic improvement over their own preparation.

Mentors characterized the requirement for field experiences that coincide with students' learning of the theoretical constructs as a significant step. They also approved the identification of a single mentor who supervises all of the student's field experiences, citing both the personal and professional benefits that can be derived from an ongoing relationship with a practitioner. One mentor, clearly pleased with the evolution of the portfolio process thus far, said it is critical that "universities develop training models like this for preservice principals which have a significant field dimension," rather than to rely on "the traditional series of classes, many of which are irrelevant."

Although mentors endorsed the revisions in the field dimensions of the program, they reported they were particularly impressed with the extensive reflective element it requires. The expectation that students demonstrate through the portfolio an ability to thoughtfully approach their work and integrate their experiences, in one mentor's words, "will pay off in principals who are able to make sense of the chaos." Another found the conscious connection between standards and practice invaluable:

> There wasn't a single time in my whole master's program when anybody asked me if I thought I was ready to be a principal. And I couldn't tell you to this day which standards [the preservice program] used. I *am* sure nobody ever asked me to evaluate them, or whether I could implement them.

> These [ISLLC] standards *do* reflect the things that are important to me as a principal, and these guys are far more ready than I was to take on the job.

Altogether, the mentors expressed unanimous support for the transition to portfolio-based assessment and the corresponding program reforms that sustain it. Their one criticism, consistent with that of their colleagues, university-based program representatives, and professional associations, was the absence of a sustained internship, which they felt should occur prior to the construction of the portfolio and would allow students to extend what they had learned through the 32 required field experiences they had completed in conjunction with their coursework (appendix B). Fiscal limitations presently preclude such a possibility, but work on several fronts to make such an arrangement feasible is being done.[1]

The Students' Perspective

Though small in number, the first 51 students who have completed the portfolio assessment have provided invaluable assistance in creating an understanding of both its impact and developmental aspects. Their comments range from the deeply personal to the programmatic and contribute in a powerful way to our understanding of what constitutes meaningful preparation. Most of the comments concern the value of the collaborative process, the value of reflection and its importance to their eventual practice, the relationship between theory and practice, the value of the field experiences, and the rigor of the process of portfolio development as compared to the more conventional exit examinations.

---

1. As was noted previously, virtually all of our leadership students are employed full time, most of them as classroom teachers. Freeing them from their teaching responsibilities for even a brief period involves significant cost to the school district that must hire a full-time substitute during their absence. We recently received a generous grant from the Wallace Funds to field test an internship model during which the grant would provide monies to the districts to secure substitute teachers. Data from this pilot program suggest that even a one-month internship, during which the intern works full time as an administrator, is sufficient to permit an informed decision concerning whether to pursue the principalship or remain in the classroom. Although we fully agree with others who advocate a longer internship period (e.g., Hackmann, Schmitt-Oliver, & Tracy, 2002; Morgan, Hertzog, & Gibbs, 2002), these findings are promising in light of fiscal concerns that presently mitigate against that ideal. The full report was available in the fall of 2003 to policymakers and legislators in an attempt to demonstrate that such an experience is not only desirable but necessary in the realistic preparation of school leaders. The report to the Ventures in Leadership initiative will also be available through the Wallace Funds or from the author.

In her discussion of teacher portfolios, Lyons (1998) submits that perhaps the "most striking consequence of a portfolio process . . . is the creation of a new norm . . . that is, making public discussion and debate about what constitutes good teaching" (p. 250). The students who are among the first of our portfolio principals seem to agree. A significant number of the graduates addressed the issue of collaboration, of engaging in the process in the company of their peers, mentors, and faculty members. One suggested that this shared process was her "first real experience with the concept of collegiality," saying that although she was familiar with the construct, she'd "never really seen it work." Another characterized the process, particularly the capstone course during which portfolio construction was the primary focus, as a "support network," expressing gratitude to his peers for their "patience" and "open-mindedness." Lyons's (1998) work with teachers suggests that such a position is understandable:

> For many teachers, their most prized ways of doing things have never been shared with others, and certainly have rarely been subjected to the insights or probings of critical friends. Thus, the portfolio process opens to scrutiny and interrogation debate about what constitutes good practice and sustains the conversation over a long period of time. An emerging characteristic of a teacher as a professional is this ability to articulate, evaluate, engage in, and respond to criticism about teaching, their own practice, and student learning. (p. 251)

Students seem to have recognized that it is not only the ongoing documentation of and reflection on their work that has rendered their preservice preparation different from that of their faculty and mentors, but rather the open and collaborative conditions under which that work was completed and shared. One noted how different such a model was from his undergraduate experience wherein "any kind of collaboration other than assigned group work was frowned on . . . if you wanted to talk about an individual assignment, it was like you were trying to steal ideas or something."

Another addressed the degree to which ongoing collaboration with her peers prepared her for the openness of the portfolio symposium and the experience of interacting with faculty and practicing administrators:

> As I reflect back over the work required, I'm thinking not only of the assignments and field experiences, and of course the portfolio presentation,

> but of the environment in which I did that work . . . of the collaboration with my peers, which made it easier to share my personal thoughts about what kind of leaders schools need. It was kind of intimidating to talk about that with faculty and mentors in the room, but having the experience of talking through it with my peers made it easier to discuss in a more open forum. [The portfolio symposium] was sort of like a professional conference, where everyone's on the same level and discussing important issues about leadership. We shouldn't have to wait until we're principals and going to conferences to talk to other principals about what constitutes effective administration.

Students also addressed the issue of how engaging in critical self-examination on an ongoing basis has contributed to their internalizing the process—to believing in its importance to their continued professional growth.

> I think too often people, especially in the education field, do not take the time to self-evaluate. Instead they get caught up in doing the same old things or are too busy criticizing others. It is my belief that until we do evaluate ourselves and are able to see our deficiencies, we won't improve to become our personal best. I do not plan to stop evaluating myself now that my portfolio is completed. Instead, creating the portfolio has conditioned my mind into constantly thinking about where I am, both personally and professionally, and where I want to be.

Some examined directly the issue of theoretical concerns, both as they relate to their growing awareness of the place of theory in preservice preparation and the questions surrounding the relationship of theory to practice. One student recalled a classroom discussion he found enlightening:

> I remember early in the program we talked about the definition of theory—"a set of assumptions which guide practice"—and I remember wondering why I didn't know that. I have a previous master's degree, but I don't recall any examination of the purpose of theory. We *did* a lot of theory, but there was never any discussion of *why*. If I'd known [that] the reason we were talking about it was that these are the ideas that can shape or explain what I do in the classroom, I might've paid more attention. I might've even figured out why I do what I do when I teach. Do-

ing the field experiences while we were covering them in class brought home to me what I was doing. It's way more useful than just learning a list of theories and their names. What's the point in that?

Others seem to share that sentiment, one noting that "I didn't realize that when we talked about theory, we could be talking about our own approaches to doing things. I thought theories had to have names or titles, or be developed by somebody well-known. You know, like in a textbook or something." Understanding that the assumptions under which she operated, which guide her own practice, constituted her own theoretical bearings "was a revelation." Another, pleased to find his interest in equity issues reflected in the thinking of the critical theorists, thought it "great to finally have a perspective I can name."

All the students mentioned the field experiences and the accompanying folios, which required reflective examinations of the experiences. Some appreciated the more functionalist elements, characterizing them as "invaluable learning opportunities" that "help [us] enter the principalship with at least some familiarity of the tasks required." Their reflections uniformly addressed the value of "knowing what to expect," and many noted as well that learning the vast number of things that could place demands on their time "was a really eye-opening experience. No wonder principals have no time to reflect."

Another addressed the value of the field reflection requirement as a "chance to really focus on whether there is a gap between the theory we study and the field experiences we were doing," pointing out that it "helped [her] understand why theory's useful." She went on to explain that she was referring not only to the perceived discrepancy between preservice preparation and actual practice, but to "understanding why I [choose to] focus on the things I do." The process of identifying the theoretical underpinnings of her own work helped her to explain "why [she] found some things really important and others less so," and "forced [her] to recognize that while [she] considered certain obligations trivial, they still have to be dealt with."

Several students echoed the sentiment that the effort to connect theory and practice by embedding the field experiences in their coursework was "enormously helpful" to them, one noting that she was certain that "if [she'd] waited 'til the end of the program to do some of this stuff, [she'd] have forgotten why." One of her peers took a different approach. Although he agreed that the opportunity to "test-drive" the theory(ies) under discussion proved helpful in discerning their practical applications, he pointed out the contribution the field experiences made to his classroom work:

> I agree, like everyone says, that test-driving what we're doing in class in a real school environment is a great learning experience. But I kind of see it from another perspective too. Doing the field experiences helped me understand what we were talking about [in class]. It made more sense—or when it didn't, I could kind of figure out why.

Perhaps the most persuasive confirmation that distributing the field experiences throughout the program was valuable to students examined the professional relationship that had developed between one student and his mentor. His observation validated the kind of "mind-to-mind" (Geltner, 1993) contact we were hoping to encourage, in spite of our inability to provide a sustained apprentice-like experience:

> I really don't know if I'd have made it through this without [my mentor]. I remember when I interviewed him for the first class, I thought "I could learn a lot more from this guy than from my classes," but he helped me see the value in my classes. We'd sit down together to look at the assignment [field experience] and talk about what its purpose was, and then he'd go over it with me again after I finished it—for the reflective part. He really made me see the connections. He was my go-to guy when I didn't understand what I was supposed to be doing or why, and he was there from the start 'til the finish. Two years. If I'd only worked with him maybe during a summer class at the end, I don't think I'd know nearly as much as I do, or think I do anyway.

Finally, several students touched on the issue of the assessment itself. One noted, somewhat ruefully, that "at the outset, when I started the program, I thought the substitution of the portfolio for the comprehensive exam was going to be easier. I couldn't have been more wrong." The same student, however, reported her satisfaction with the process:

> The construction of the portfolio proved to have a positive effect on me. Although not having a real example to follow created some stress, once I completed it, it felt like a real achievement. The creation of the port-

> folio allowed me to really analyze myself—what I think, what I know, and what I need to find out. Beyond a standardized test, the portfolio gave me the opportunity to be an individual. It was a display of my personal best.

Another also addressed the difference she saw between the traditional comprehensive exam and the process of constructing her portfolio, noting the extent to which the latter required her to analyze her program of study in a holistic fashion:

> It all finally came together in the end. When [the capstone course] started, I think we were all pretty much at a loss. No one quite understood what was expected of us in terms of taking a theoretical stance on the work we'd previously completed. After a lot of reflection, though, and a lot of collaboration, it all started to come together—each course, each field experience, and each reflection, all contributing to our professional growth in a way we could actually see. No test can do that.

That, perhaps, is the most important among the students' observations. If students are unable to connect their experiences through sustained reflection, the portfolio is little more than a new collection technique. For the process to be a meaningful one, students have to understand its constructivist foundation and embrace its requisite reflective dimensions. One student expressed it clearly: "No one else can make me the principal I want to be. I have to do that myself."

LESSONS LEARNED

As was noted in the preface, the preservice principal portfolio is something of an organic phenomenon. Although the principles to which the leadership studies program is committed provide a stable foundation for the program of study, the point of an assessment approach that relies on constructivist learning and reflective thinking is to encourage all those involved in its implementation to reflect on their experiences, question their practices, attempt to comprehend their effects, and to either reinforce or reform them. If this is what we expect of students, we should expect no less of ourselves; if assessment for them is ongoing and integrated, so should it be for the program.

That conviction has led to a review of the entirety of the portfolio process—coursework, field experiences, and reflective assignments—on a semester-by-semester basis. Even before our first graduates entered the capstone course, a lot of time had been devoted to refining the experience based on student evaluations and faculty observations. Although chapter 4 addressed some of these issues in a broad fashion, there are some matters that should be addressed in a more specific way. Many of these are operational; others, more complex in terms of remedy, are conceptual.

Operational Lessons

Operational lessons, for the most part, were identified through student evaluations. Almost without exception, their comments have been both relevant and insightful.

The portfolio "mentality" has to permeate the program. Students who just completed their programs noted that aside from the intense attention the portfolio process receives in the introductory and capstone courses, there is sometimes little to remind them of its existence. One student, pointing out that the assessments for her field experiences rarely appeared in her records on the portfolio website unless she contacted the professor of record to ask where they were, wondered "whether faculty [other than those who teach the introductory and capstone courses] even know about the portfolio." Although faculty *do* know, since all were an integral part of realigning course content to accommodate the process and attended and expressed their satisfaction with the capstone presentations, it does appear there is more to be done in terms of emphasizing the ongoing nature of the process.

Concerning the field experiences, for example, although students are advised they will need to maintain their documentation for eventual use in constructing their portfolios, it appears those are seen more as discrete course assignments than elements in an ongoing, program-long process. One student recommended that "the field experiences . . . be assigned and discussed in terms of the [ISLLC] standards which provide the framework for the portfolio. Otherwise, they're just another assignment." It might be helpful if faculty were to make clearer for students the relationships between required field experiences and the program principles/standards. Although those connections may seem self-evident to us, as do many of the assignments we make, it is true that those links aren't always visible to students.

Such oversights should not be seen as an attempt to subvert the process. Rather it is likely that faculty, accustomed to a broad degree of autonomy in their individual courses, merely need to conceptualize in a more conscious way the holistic nature of the portfolio assessment. All of us, whether participating in an ongoing assessment method or not, generally see ourselves as parts of a larger project (i.e., the student's program of study). That vision, however, tends to be more abstract than concrete. For an assessment approach such as this to function holistically, it is imperative that faculty be attuned to it in a conscious fashion. That extends from the smaller operational details, such as requiring students to enter their reflections on the portfolio website or teachers routinely submitting assessments at the end of the term, to ensuring that the connections between coursework/field experiences and the standards that provide the scaffolding for the program are visible to students.

Reflective writings may need to be systematized. As discussed in chapter 4, it was decided that it was best not to connect reflective writings to any particular courses. Since the standards themselves are woven throughout the program, determining a locus for them seemed arbitrary; and, we reasoned, part of becoming a principal is learning to organize one's work and time. Thus, the submission of these essays was left to the students on an independent basis. Human nature being what it is, however, most students tended to neglect them until they realized they could not enroll in the capstone course unless all six had been completed, submitted, and assessed. The result was a veritable deluge of reflective essays to be read by the faculty in an extremely narrow time frame.

A majority of the students who completed the program to date have recommended that the suggested time lines for submission of the essays be replaced with a mandatory deadline for each. Since accommodating that recommendation seems contrary to the desire to see students function autonomously, there has been continued resistance to attaching them to a course and essentially transferring responsibility to the faculty. However, firmer deadlines have been considered, perhaps taking the same approach that is taken to enrollment in the capstone course (i.e., requiring the essays be submitted at intervals throughout the program, perhaps at the completion of every 6 credit hours, and delaying further enrollment until their submission; see appendix H).

Electronic issues mustn't be underestimated. Although it was recognized that working in an electronic environment could present difficulties for some students, the level of stress it would produce in those who feel less than comfortable with emerging technologies had been underestimated. The average age of the student body in the graduate school is nearly 39; they are generally people who would be less comfortable with a multimedia format than the traditional 18-year-old college student. Although the migration to an online course delivery system meant that students had to make some adjustments in how they interacted with faculty and course content, it was understood that navigating the Internet and constructing a multimedia presentation of their own were two entirely different things.

In an effort to address that issue, arrangements were made to allow students to have unlimited access to the university's computer resources and appointments with computer services staff who worked with them to assemble their portfolio presentations. Still, the student evaluations from the capstone course suggested that some more formal training in certain presentation programs (e.g., Netscape Composer, FrontPage, or PowerPoint) would have been helpful. The staff from the computer services unit were asked to prepare some training modules that they would conduct in the early weeks of the capstone course, and the possibility of having them conduct some stand-alone workshops at various times during the semester, which would be open to students at any point in their programs, was explored.

Some students also raised another issue related to the media component of the portfolio presentation, growing perhaps from their inexperience in the electronic domain. They were concerned that the content of their portfolios might be diminished by a less than sophisticated media presentation: "Pretty graphics and nice music don't prove a person's capable of being an effective school leader," noted one.

It is important that students be reminded of both the conceptual and utilitarian reasons for the electronic format (i.e., its consistency with constructivist principles and its available options, which are either impossible or impracticable in conventional portfolios). It is also necessary to assure them that the media elements of their portfolios will neither compensate for an unacceptable presentation nor impair an exceptional one. Although creativity in the multimedia dimension can enhance an acceptable presentation, it cannot eclipse a poor one.

Appropriate rubrics are imperative. Despite our efforts to construct assessment rubrics that are preordinate (i.e., which make clear to the students what will qualify as an acceptable folio entry or portfolio presentation), this issue remains a troubling one. In the same way that the difference between a conventional "A" and "B" sometimes remains a deep mystery to students, the development of rubrics that sufficiently reveal the criteria on which a particular item will be assessed is problematic. As was noted in the discussion of implementation challenges, the issue of interrater reliability is difficult to resolve, as is the tendency to want to standardize any such instrument in the interest of fairness and validity.

This is not, however, a novel phenomenon. As long ago as 1921, Edward Thorndike offered this response to criticism of some newly developed standardized tests:

> It will be said that learning should be for learning's sake, that too much attention is given already in this country to marks, prizes, degrees and the like, that students work for marks rather than for real achievement. . . . Students will work for marks and degrees if we have them. We can have none, or we can have such as are worth working for. (p. 378)

Clearly, assessing student portfolios requires what Wolf (1998) calls "a new kind of clinical judgment" (p. 49)—one that is far more complex than the simple examining of a student's work to ensure it conforms to a prescribed standard or expectation. Equally clear is the difficulty of constructing an assessment instrument that takes into account that complexity without undermining it by excessive standardization. We are, in fact, on the third revision of our assessment rubrics, each brought about by recognition that its predecessor was sufficiently ambiguous as to merit reconsideration.

Mabry (1999), in an examination of rubrics for assessing students' composition skills, points out that since evidence of validity has always been difficult to achieve, assessment professionals have been inclined to concentrate more on providing proof of reliability; but even establishing reliability in performance-based assessments "is fiendishly difficult to achieve." She recommends that the measurement community "reconsider the importance of reliability where it is attained at the expense of validity" (p. 680).

We share Mabry's conviction that buying reliability at the expense of validity defeats the purpose of authentic assessment. We also, as was indicated in chapter 2 on epistemological concerns, agree with Schulman (1998) that as new forms of assessment are implemented, even previous measures for determining validity will likely be found inadequate. Our emphasis in the portfolio project thus conforms more to Schulman's recommendation for "consequential validity," explained as "ensuring that the manner in which it is deployed improves the quality of [educational leadership] and opportunities for becoming better [school leaders]" (p. 30). It is this we keep in mind as we attempt to arrive at assessment rubrics that are appropriate.

Conceptual Lessons

Although the operational insights were primarily provided by students' evaluations, what has been learned conceptually about the process of portfolio-based assessment has been the result of both student and faculty observations. These will take some time to work out, but their resolution is considered critical to the success of the project.

The nature of self-assessment needs to be emphasized throughout the program. Although the term is ubiquitous in program materials, it seems to have been largely irrelevant to students until they enrolled in the capstone course. That is the point at which the real questions began. Students in the capstone course complained that they needed more guidance in terms of the process. Isn't there a template I can follow? What kind of artifacts should I choose? Which software/media program should I use? What kind of organizational pattern should I follow? Should I move through the standards in order or as I interpret their importance? How much should I say during the presentation and how much should I "show"?

These kinds of questions were not surprising. For the most part, students' prior educational experiences have led them to expect that explicit directions will be provided. Understanding that their experience with assessment has been to associate the process with evaluation conducted by an external agent or agency, primarily in the form of tests, their pleas for specific directions were both anticipated and understandable.

On the ground that giving them a template would have undermined the very constructivist element we had sought to emphasize, however, the temptation to standardize the process was resisted. Once the students realized they were on their own, so to speak, they began the gradual transition to training a critical eye on their own learning and how they might best demonstrate it in an independent fashion. Their comments subsequent to the portfolio symposium reflected an understanding of why we thought it important to elicit that independence:

> While I was thinking about what to say in my program evaluation, I'd first intended to suggest that you provide samples of our portfolios to the students who are entering the capstone course next. However, I changed my mind on that because this would hinder you in getting such a variety of excellent presentations as we experienced [in the symposium]. Giving people an example might result in too much similarity. Personal growth and development can only be demonstrated from a personal perspective.

Others agreed. Although most found it stressful to an extent, they seem to have recognized the value of taking the individual approach:

> I think we all started out approaching the creation of the portfolio very similar to the way we approach standardized testing in public schools—anticipating it would be stressful! My own students put so much pressure on themselves because they think they aren't going to pass, that they do poorly on the test because of the stress. I spent most of the duration of the program dreading the end because of the portfolio, when instead it proved to be such a rewarding experience. Students need to see it as a celebration of themselves, and understand that it's far less stressful to demonstrate what they *do* know than to worry they'll be asked something they *don't*.

Clearly, once they'd completed their presentations in the capstone symposium, students came to understand that by imposing a standardized format the development of their own professional judgment would have been impeded. The question is how we can help them comprehend that concept prior to the culminating experience in the program; how we can begin to cultivate that developmental process sooner?

If self-assessment is, in fact, at the heart of what is an ongoing and integrated process, we need to ensure its presence is felt from the beginning of students' programs of study to the end. It is likely we will undertake an in-depth review of coursework, field experiences, and reflections to discern how we might make the element of self-assessment more central to their completion.

Reflection would be more easily assessed if it were a unitary phenomenon. As Schon (1987) points out, however, reflection is not a unitary phenomenon. His distinction, discussed in chapter 2, between reflection-*on*-action, which is retrospective, and reflection-*in*-action, where thinking and doing coincide, is consistent with the work of Ross (1990) and Sparks-Langer and Colton (1991), who refer to these processes as "technical reflection." Technical reflection, given what we know about the daily demands on the principal's time, is central to our understanding of the qualities necessary to the successful practice of educational leadership, and it is promoted accordingly through the portfolio process.

Both the construction of the portfolio and its subsequent presentation in the public symposium give students ample opportunity to develop and demonstrate their ability to engage in reflection-on-action as well as reflection-in-action. Both forms are relative easy to recognize and, if evaluation of such subjective undertakings can ever be construed as a straightforward undertaking, reasonably simple to assess. The extent to which a student has mastered the art of technical reflection can be detected largely in its presence or absence in the capstone presentation. A significant level of reflecting *on* what they have done and learned is necessary in order to even begin the construction of their portfolios. Likewise, the presentation of their work in the symposium is visible evidence of the degree to which they have learned to reflect *in* action.

Based on the research (reviewed in chapter 2) that suggests that the managerial role has continued to dominate principals' daily routine and that the vast majority of their time is given over to preventing small problems from turning into big ones, evidence that principals in the preservice phase of their careers comprehend both the expectations for and processes of technical reflection is encouraging. It suggests that they have, in fact, begun to develop a thoughtful orientation to their work. But what of Bleakley's (1999) "third form"? What of "reflection-*as*-action"? How can we discern whether a student, or anyone else for that matter, has internalized the process? How can we tell whether thinking about one's thinking has become second nature or whether its demonstration will endure only until the capstone course has ended? That, it turns out, is a most complex issue; but it is one that deserves our attention.

Our premise has been that the portfolio process, resting on a constructivist foundation that conceives of reflection as essential to the student's continuing professional development, will lay the groundwork for the extension of that behavior to practice. Learning does not stop because formal education has ended. As Palmer (1997) points out, "the most practical thing we can achieve in any kind of work is insight into what is happening inside us as we do it. The more familiar we are with our inner terrain, the more surefooted our [work]—and living—becomes" (p. 21).

Whether learning to know themselves through systematic reflection on their student experiences does, in fact, sustain our portfolio principals in their lives as administrators cannot, of course, be determined until graduates of the program are actually involved in the practice of educational administration. Some suggestions on how this phenomenon might be examined follow.

REFLEXIVE EVALUATION

Any new assessment model must eventually address the issue of reflexive evaluation (i.e., How does one assess the assessment model?). The measure of consequential validity, raised in chapter 2, is for us a primary criterion in such an evaluation. If portfolio assessment is alleged to represent an improvement in the preparation of school administrators, one that conceives of constructivist learning and a reflective orientation as a means to a more effective administrative practice, we have to discern what difference it makes in the lives of practitioners. Such an interest requires an inclusive assessment method. The literature focusing on alternative assessment processes has changed the way evaluators approach their work. A substantial and growing body of research advocates that evaluation be conducted in a way that represents the subjective realities of those involved in the process (Guba & Lincoln, 1994; Lather, 1992;

Lincoln, 1994; Mertens, 1995, 1998; Ryan, 1998; Stanfield & Dennis, 1993). That research confirms Fullan's (1991) observation that chief among the reasons so many reforms fail is a corresponding failure on the part of advocates to take into account "the phenomenology of change" (i.e., the lived experiences of those who participate in the reform). Because the primary justification for the implementation of the reforms discussed herein was the improvement of the preservice experience, there is a deep interest in seeing them succeed.

There are reasons beyond ensuring the success of our programmatic revisions, however, to take an inclusive approach to their evaluation. First, we share Schwandt's (1989) belief that the inclusion of multiple voices in the evaluation process is a way to build a sense of community among participants; to create a set of shared values that can serve to anchor relationships. Because part of the rationale for the reforms we implemented was to reduce the distance between the university and schools, we sought the input of constituents from both environments from the outset. We took seriously the suggestions of students, former and current, and practicing administrators in reshaping the dimensions of the preservice experience. Involving them in the evaluation process is a logical extension of that approach.

Second, inclusive evaluation methods are consistent with both the constructivist and reflective aims of the project. The portfolio process itself is designed to offer multiple opportunities for self-assessment, for synthesizing what has been learned and accommodating that knowledge in a meaningful way to enhance the usefulness of the experience for students. Those opportunities are realized in conditions that invite deliberate and thoughtful consideration of the elements of that experience. We want to bring those same practices to our programmatic assessment.

What we envision is a collaborative and deliberative process through which those involved—faculty, students, and mentors—jointly construct an understanding of the extent to which the portfolio project has been successful in meeting program goals. As Lincoln (1995) cautions, such approaches are necessarily complex given their interest in subjects who resist uniform measures:

> This will make our professional judgments harder, but it has the potential to make our research more locally useable, as we might perhaps tailor our criteria to the community [affected by it], or, even better, permit criteria to grow indigenously as a natural consequence of the inquiry effort. (p. 288)

Certainly, using a criterion such as "improved practice" or allowing appropriate criteria to emerge from the evaluation effort itself will make our programmatic assessment more difficult. Ultimately, however, it stands to make the program both more valuable to students and more responsive to the needs of schools. Surely that is worth the effort.

LIVING WITH AN ORGANIC PROCESS

Extensive research on the change process proves that real, enduring reform is incremental, not revolutionary. The implementation of the portfolio project is, we believe, one such change. Although we have undertaken substantial revision in the dimensions of this program of study in order to accommodate the transition from conventional to alternative assessment, none has been especially radical. Most, in fact, such as ensuring that course content is aligned with accreditation standards or redistributing the field experiences in order to connect them more closely with their theoretical underpinnings, would have been accomplished eventually with or without the change in assessment approach.

The most difficult aspect of our reformed approach to assessment, perhaps, has been learning to live with what is essentially an organic process. Self-assessment by nature resists standardization, and we continue to wrestle with the transition to evaluation by rubric. We also continue to refine the various elements of the preservice principal portfolio as we find need to reexamine them. As both faculty and students began to question the need for assessment of course folios, for instance, we determined that asking professors both to submit grades and record a separate evaluation of coursework in the students' portfolio records was, in fact, duplicative. Although students still maintain their course folios for purposes of having access to the work for portfolio construction and for submission on their exit disks, we no longer feature them on the students' portfolio records web page.

We fully expect that these kinds of revisions will continue as we learn from students how we might facilitate their grasp of self-assessment, as we learn from faculty how we might strengthen program quality, and as we learn from schools how we might be more responsive to their needs. If it is true that the greatest threat to programmatic relevance is inflexibility, the dynamic nature of this process is surely a healthy sign.

APPENDIX A

ISLLC Standards for School Leaders

Standard 1: Vision	A school administrator is an educational leader who promotes the success of all students by facilitating the development, articulation, implementation, and stewardship of a vision of learning that is shared and supported by the school community.
Standard 2: Scholarship	A school administrator is an educational leader who promotes the success of all students by advocating, nurturing, and sustaining a school culture and instructional program conducive to student learning and staff professional growth.
Standard 3: Stewardship	A school administrator is an educational leader who promotes success of all students by ensuring management of the organization, operations, and resources for a safe, efficient, and effective learning environment.
Standard 4: Collaboration	A school administrator is an educational leader who promotes the success of all students by collaborating with families and community members, responding to diverse community interests and needs, and mobilizing community resources.
Standard 5: Integrity	A school administrator is an educational leader who promotes the success of all students by acting with integrity, fairness, and in an ethical manner.
Standard 6: Context	A school administrator is an educational leader who promotes the success of all students by understanding, responding to, and influencing the larger political, social, economic, legal, and cultural context.

Source: Interstate School Leaders Licensure Consortium (1996).

APPENDIX B

Field Experience Chart

Course Number	*Course Title*	*Field Experience*
LS 500	Introduction to School Leadership	Conduct interview with field mentor.
LS 506	Planning, Research, and Evaluation	Analyze data for a school improvement plan.
LS 510	The Principalship	Develop a school budget; prepare a plan for correcting identified safe facility issues; develop a school schedule; and demonstrate the use of administrative software.
LS 512	Curriculum Leadership	Assess the alignment of a curricular area; evaluate the content/design of an educational software program; and participate in the development of an individualized educational plan (IEP) and in a school-based assistance team (SBAT) activity.
LS 515	Instructional Leadership	Observe and evaluate a classroom teacher and write a teacher improvement plan.
LS 520	Administration of Elementary, Middle, and Secondary Schools	Analyze a facility for developmentally appropriate instruction; plan an extracurricular activity; and

(*continued*)

Course Number	*Course Title*	*Field Experience*
		participate in and document a student discipline procedure.
LS 530	Human Relations	Complete a personal leadership profile.
LS 550	Schools as Systems	Attend and analyze a state or county school board meeting; plan and conduct a principal interview; and analyze a system organizational chart.
LS 600	School Personnel Administration	Write a job posting; construct a staff development plan; conduct a job interview; and develop a school service personnel schedule.
LS 610	Leadership for School Improvement	Write a school vision/mission statement, and evaluate a school improvement plan (SIP).
LS 630	School and Community Relations	Analyze a community survey; develop a community involvement plan; plan and coordinate a school–community meeting; develop and disseminate a community newsletter.
LS 675	Legal and Policy Issues	Critique an educational policy; analyze an employee grievance; and analyze a safe schools plan.

APPENDIX C

Field Experience Rubric

Assessment Area	*Exceptional*	*Acceptable*	*Unacceptable*
Entries Assignment(s)	Field experience is conducted in a manner that exhibits a thoroughness in both understanding and execution of each element involved. Initiative is shown through student's going beyond requirements of assignment (e.g., consulting and citing of additional resources, displaying work in an innovative fashion, etc.)	Field experience is conducted in a manner that demonstrates understanding of the elements involved. Execution meets assignment criteria, demonstrating proficiency and recognition of the purpose of the experience.	Field experience does not meet assignment criteria, and shows little or no evidence of either proficiency or understanding of the purpose of the experience.
Field Experience Reflection	Reflection on experience shows an ability to recognize and synthesize propositional and procedural knowledge. Tensions between	Reflection on experience demonstrates a recognition of propositional and procedural elements involved. Reflection adequately	Reflection on experience shows minimal understanding of either propositional or procedural elements involved. Discussion of impact of

(*continued*)

Assessment Area	*Exceptional*	*Acceptable*	*Unacceptable*
	theoretical suppositions and practical application are noted, and approaches for reconciling them explored. Impact on student learning is discussed in depth.	addresses impact of experience on student's learning.	experience on student's learning is absent.
Presentation/ Mechanics	Documentation of experience and subsequent reflection display excellent organizational skills (i.e., strong introduction, smooth transitions, and comprehensive conclusion), presenting ideas both cogently and with attention to detail. No mechanical errors are present.	Documentation of experience and subsequent reflection display adequate organizational skills (i.e., ideas flow logically from one to the other), presenting ideas in a clear fashion with few mechanical errors.	Documentation of experience and/or subsequent reflection do(es) not conform to expectations for graduate work. Ideas are poorly organized, and presentation contains multiple mechanical errors.

APPENDIX D

Reflective Essay Rubric

Assessment Area	*Exceptional*	*Acceptable*	*Unacceptable*
Entry, Vision, Scholarship, Stewardship, Collaboration, Integrity, Context	Treatment of subject is thorough and creative, illuminating in depth the student's attitudes, values, and beliefs. Examples are insightful and supportive of positions taken and discussion is framed within the context of leadership. Student's recognition of the subjectivity of her/his positions is explicitly addressed.	Treatment of subject is adequate and includes an examination of student's attitudes, values, and beliefs. Examples support positions taken and relate to the practice of leadership.	Treatment of subject is superficial and relies primarily on a generic approach. Evidence of students' attitudes, values, and beliefs is absent, and relationship between examples and the practice of leadership is not addvessed.
Presentation/ Mechanics	Ideas are expressed both cogently and with attention to detail. Presentation is enhanced by superior organization, and no mechanical errors are present.	Ideas are expressed clearly and flow in a logical fashion. There are few mechanical errors.	Entries do not conform to expectations for graduate work. Ideas are poorly articulated and presentation includes multiple

APPENDIX E

Portfolio Rubric

Assessment Area	*Exceptional*	*Acceptable*	*Unacceptable*
Conceptualization	Selection of entries is carefully made to demonstrate in-depth comprehension of program principles and ISLLC standards and dispositions, as well as a high degree of insight regarding their interdependence with professional practice. Entries include elements from each of the folio categories, and illustrate a clear and insightful recognition of their interrelationships.	Selection of entries demonstrates knowledge of program principles and ISLLC standards and dispositions, and an adequate understanding of their interdependence with professional practice. Entries include elements from each of the folio categories, and illustrate recognition of their interrelationships.	Selection of entries reflects insufficient evidence of knowledge of program principles and/or ISLLC standards and dispositions, and/or an inadequate understanding of their interdependence with professional practice. Folio categories are not adequately represented, and there is insufficient recognition of their interrelationships.
Coherence	Portfolio is enhanced by adherence to a thematic framework grounded in	Student's leadership philosophy provides thematic unity for portfolio, allowing for logical	No visible thematic framework exists to explain relationships between and

(*continued*)

Assessment Area	*Exceptional*	*Acceptable*	*Unacceptable*
	student's leadership philosophy and reinforced by selection of entries. Theme provides a unique perspective that allows for creative development of ideas.	development of ideas.	among entries. Development of ideas is vague, and student's leadership philosophy is unclear.
Personal/ Professional Growth	Portfolio demonstrates sustained reflection and critical thought. Assimilation of knowledge, both propositional and procedural, is central to the presentation, providing evidence of reflection and constructivist principles (i.e., the congruency or incompatibility of new knowledge with prior knowledge is expressed, and the process of reinforcement or reconciliation is explicitly addressed by the student). Presentation addresses how development of portfolio contributed to personal/ professional growth.	Portfolio demonstrates evidence of reflection and critical thought. A degree of insightfulness is apparent in the student's work, and elements of reflection and constructivist principles are recognizable. Presentation addresses process of portfolio development and rationale for selection of entries.	Portfolio demonstrates little evidence of reflection or critical thought. Presentation addresses neither the process of portfolio development nor reasons for inclusion of selected entries. There is little evidence of either reflection or constructivist principles.

(*continued*)

Assessment Area	*Exceptional*	*Acceptable*	*Unacceptable*
Symposium Presentation	Ideas are expressed cogently and with attention to detail. Portfolio and presentation are enhanced by creative application of a range of multimedia options, and there are no mechanical (i.e., grammatical) errors to detract from the presentation.	Ideas are expressed in a clear fashion. Connections between and among portfolio entries are made clear through logical use of multimedia options and there are few mechanical (i.e., grammatical) errors.	Presentation does not conform to the expectations for graduate work. Multimedia options are confusing or absent, resulting in a portfolio of discrete entries. Ideas are poorly articulated and multiple mechanical (i.e., grammatical) errors detract from the presentation.

APPENDIX F

Writing Prompts

STANDARD 1: VISION

Organizational consultant Margaret Wheatley (1994) talks about a number of "incoherent companies" with which she'd worked in the aftermath of massive reorganizations or leveraged buyouts. She describes them as businesses that had lost all sense of purpose other than basic survival, and speaks of the inevitability of low morale on the part of employees whose futures had become uncertain.

There was, however, a small cadre of employees whose behavior puzzled her, whose ongoing energy and creativity were clearly at odds with the prevailing attitude of most who continued to work. Her first assumption was that they were in denial, but her conversations with them revealed that what they were doing was more than merely ignoring what their fellow employees perceived as their unavoidable fate. Wheatley's assessment of their unusual behavior is that it was derived from their investing their work with purpose, from taking the time to create a meaning for their work that transcended the existing organizational circumstances.

Viktor Frankl (1959), as Wheatley notes, makes much the same point in his classic *Man's Search for Meaning*, pointing out that those who survived the horror of Nazi concentration camps were those who were able to see beyond their current circumstances. Those who could conceive of a life beyond their present suffering, who could create a vision of their futures, gave purpose to their existence. Their own contemplation and their conversations with confidantes about their struggles and their mutual plans for survival lent coherence to their daily adversity. It is vision that gives purpose to our behavior. It is the catalyst that compels us to act. It is both inspiration and motivation. Shale (1995) describes it as a way of structuring the future—of embracing our desires so completely that they become our experiences.

As you prepare to write your reflective piece on this issue, you might consider grounding it in what your own leadership vision is, keeping in mind that the development of vision entails more than simple identification of a leadership style. It is grounded in, or evidence of, your beliefs and values in action. What are those beliefs? Those values? How or from what were they derived? Are they deep enough to lend a discernible pattern to practice? What are their inherent possibilities?

Wheatley (1994) also discusses the importance of leaders who can help to create a shared vision, who can give voice and form to the organization's search for meaning. Reminding us that we all want to know the "why" of what's going on, she argues that it is the leaders who can work with us to answer that question of whom we cherish. Nanus (1996) agrees, pointing out that many considered great leaders in history (e.g., Jefferson, Lincoln, Gandhi) were successful precisely because they were capable of articulating and sharing their visions, and asking if they were worth supporting. Effective organizations, Nanus says, are those in which individuals are invited to participate in the development and implementation of the vision or to which they're attracted because the vision is compatible with their own.

Vision serves as a reference point that allows both leaders and participants to make decisions and act, but it is the leader on whom the articulation responsibility falls. DePree (1989), in fact, identifies the sharing of vision as the "first responsibility" of the leader (p. 9). Sashkin (1995) sees it as a two-step process: expressing the vision and explaining the vision to others (p. 404). You may wish to reflect on what your vision is, how your vision may be "expressed," and how it may be shared with your school communities. What happens if your vision is at odds with the vision(s) of the school community? How then might a vision be constructed that is meaningful for everyone involved? How can it be made the primary focus of everyone involved? Dess and Miller (1993) believe that vision "becomes tangible as a mission statement" (p. 25). If you were to attempt to convert your vision into a mission statement, how would it read?

STANDARD 2: SCHOLARSHIP

It was in 1967 that Robert Schaefer proposed his concept of the school as a center of inquiry. While his model is primarily concerned with the teaching profession, it has significant implications for administrative practice as well. It was his intent to transform the school from a center for the distribution of knowledge produced elsewhere to a center for the production of knowledge itself:

> We can no longer afford to conceive of the schools simply as distribution centers for dispensing cultural orientations, information, and knowledge developed by other social units. The complexities of teaching and learning in formal classrooms have become so formidable and the intellectual demands upon the systems so enormous that the school must be much more than a place of instruction. It must be a center of inquiry—a producer as well as a transmitter of knowledge. (p. 1)

Now, more than 30 years later, those complexities are even more profound. While we've learned much in past three decades, there is much remaining to be discovered, analyzed, applied, and accepted or rejected. Reducing teachers to mere dispensers of information and students to vessels wastes the potential of both, as reform efforts in teacher education acknowledge. It is equally wasteful to reduce principals to building managers whose primary focus is administrative matters at the expense of their intellectual capital as well, yet that's largely what's occurred. Instructional leadership is subordinated to the administrative crisis of the moment.

Linda Darling-Hammond (1993), in an argument against the implementation of a national curriculum, objects to efforts to make the current system of schooling "more efficient" by standardizing curricula and teaching practice. School reform attempts would be better served, she contends, by a focus on "building the capacity of schools and teachers to undertake tasks they have never before been called upon to accomplish" (p. 754). Such a focus, however, requires the broadening of commonly held semantic limitations (i.e., teachers must be understood to do more than teach and administrators to do more than administer). If schools are to become the kinds of centers of inquiry envisioned by Schaefer, the "learning communities" of the school reform literature, it is imperative that the knowledge potential of administrators, teachers, and students be recognized, and that education be understood not as an outcome, but as an ongoing process.

Schaefer's vision of the school as a center of inquiry has a practical cast as well. If the intent of schooling is to help students become lifelong learners by developing habits for reflection and inquiry, the same must be practiced by teachers and administrators. Schlechty (1990) sees such modeling as crucial to school improvement:

> Intellectual leadership emerges in school systems when top leaders are viewed as valuing ideas, valuing the reading of books, and valuing the interchange of ideas that lead to creative formulations and innovative solutions. To establish such values, those in authority—in the superintendent's office, the union office, and the principal's office—must model what they value. (p. 101)

Sergiovanni (1996) agrees, and goes on to point out that not only will it be necessary to rethink the philosophical issues related to teaching and learning; the pragmatic issue of structuring the school day itself must be addressed. Time must be found "for teachers to reflect and to invent together as they learn and teach together" (p. 153). He warns, however, that the creation of such an environment is dependent upon administrative support:

> [T]his kind of configuration will not be possible unless more superintendents, principals and other administrators are willing to put aside the existing system of executive authority, and to replace it with collegial authority—an authority embedded in shared commitments, shared ideals, and professional responsibility. (p. 153)

The educational power of a school resides in the collective knowledge of the individuals who inhabit it. Each must be understood as having the potential to contribute to its success. You may want to consider how to best elicit this potential in your reflective essay. You may also wish to address the pragmatic dilemma raised by Sergiovanni. How might you, as principal, attempt to rearrange the school day or school year to allow teachers to find time to "reflect and invent together"? What sorts of conditions are necessary to create a school culture conducive to student learning and the ongoing professional development of faculty and administrative staff? How might they be established? What are the potential problems/trade-offs? How important is the instructional leadership role for the principal? What are its dimensions?

STANDARD 3: STEWARDSHIP

While stewardship has long been recognized as one of the functions of leadership, the source of its inclusion in the lexicon is difficult to discern. The phrase most closely associated with the trait is "servant leadership," defined by Thomas Sergiovanni (1992) as "the means by which leaders can get the necessary legitimacy to lead" (p. 124). Robert Greenleaf (1977) sees it as a kind of moral authority, and asserts that "the only authority deserving one's allegiance is that which is freely and knowingly granted by the led to the leader in response to, and in proportion to, the clearly evident servant stature of the leader" (p. 10). How does one attain "servant stature"? To clarify his definition, Greenleaf places the servant leader in the context of the servant business:

> [T]he business exists as much to provide meaningful work to the person as it exists to provide a product or service to the customer. The business then becomes a serving institution—serving those who produce and those who use. (as cited in Hickman, 1998, p. 119)

This conception of servant leadership confers a dual function: to serve those within the institution and to see that the institution itself serves its larger purpose. Those aims are achieved by embracing the traditional understanding of stewardship (i.e., faithfully executing the responsibility to manage the resources and interests of the institution on behalf of both the people who work therein and those whom the institution serves). It is an understanding predicated on trust.

Stewardship may be the most significant of the virtues a leader brings to her/his school. In the absence of trust, other such qualities as vision, scholarship, collaboration, and integrity will be necessarily difficult to either establish or sustain. How, then, is that trust derived? How does one behave in order to elicit the allegiance "which is freely and knowingly granted by the led"? If stewardship involves a process wherein others entrust to the principal certain responsibilities, what is included among them? Do they require prioritizing? Can they be shared? Should they be shared?

STANDARD 4: COLLABORATION

Ours is a culture that has for centuries divided people into leaders and followers. So much of the history we are taught in schools focuses on the "great man" who provided leadership in a time of turmoil that we know them all by name. Washington, Jefferson, and Lincoln. Roosevelt and Churchill. Gandhi and King. Lawrence Miller (1984) explains how this orientation has conditioned our views of leadership:

> Problems were always solved the same way. The Lone Ranger and his faithful Indian companion . . . came riding into town. The Lone Ranger, with his mask and mysterious identity, background, and life-style, never becomes intimate with those whom he will help. His power is partly in his mystique. Within ten minutes the Lone Ranger has understood the problem, identified who the bad guys are, and has set out to catch them. He quickly outwits the bad guys, draws his gun, and then has them behind bars. And then there was that wonderful scene at the end. The helpless victims are standing in front of their ranch or in the town square marveling at how wonderful it is now that they have been saved. . . . What did we learn from this cultural hero? 1) There is always a problem down on the ranch and someone is responsible. 2) Those who get themselves into difficulty are incapable of getting themselves out of it. . . . 3) In order to have the mystical powers needed to solve problems, you must stay behind the mask. . . . These myths are no laughing matter. Anyone who has lived within or close to our corporations knows that these myths are powerful forces in daily life. Unfortunately, none of them bears much resemblance to the real world. (pp. 54–55)

Joseph Rost (1991) believes our propensity for bisecting the population into leaders and followers has had an equally disabling effect on the latter:

> Followers, as a concept, connoted a group of people who were (1) part of the sweaty masses and therefore separated from the elites, (2) not able to act intelligently without the guidance and control of others, (3) will-

> ing to let other people (elites) take control of their lives, and (4) unproductive unless directed by others. In the leadership literature since the 1930s, therefore, followers were considered to be subordinates who were submissive and passive, and leaders were considered to be managers who were directive and active. (p. 107)

Rost objects to the inclusion of submissiveness and passivity in the leadership equation. The key element, as he sees it, is activity. Passive people, in his view, choose not to be involved, and must therefore be excluded from any discussion of leadership roles. He proposes instead a "new paradigm" of leadership in which "followers and leaders *do* leadership" (p. 109, emphasis added). Explaining that the complexities of life in the postindustrial era mean that active people may be involved in several leadership relationships simultaneously, he argues it is conceptually possible for them to be leaders only in some. In others, they will be followers:

> [Leaders and followers] are in the relationship together. They are the ones who intend real changes that reflect their mutual purposes. Metaphorically, their activities are two sides of the same coin. . . . Followers and leaders develop a relationship wherein they influence one another as well as the organization and society, and that is leadership. (p. 109)

Such a "paradigm" is wholly consistent with a collaborative orientation that accepts that all stakeholders have a legitimate role to play in the school's decision-making process, a premise regarded favorably by those involved in both the educational administration and teaching professions. How it should be implemented, however, is less clear. While there is broad agreement that the school is enriched by the active involvement of all those whose interests are joined to it, the dimensions of that involvement remain somewhat ambiguous. John Gardner (1987) illustrates the dilemma:

> Should there be a high degree of structure in the relationship—a sharp differentiation between the roles of leaders and followers, a clear hierarchy of authority . . . ? Or should the relationship be more informal, less structured, with leaders making goals clear and then letting constituents help determine the way of proceeding? Should there be an atmosphere of

> discipline, constraints, controls . . . or should there be autonomy, individual responsibility, and freedom for growth, with the leader in the role of nurturer, supporter, listener, helper? Should the leader focus on the job to be done . . . or should the leader be concerned primarily with the people performing the task, with their needs, their morale, their growth? (p. 5)

Gardner goes on to say that there are no simple answers; that there are merely complicated answers "hedged by conditions and exceptions." One of the reasons for this inability to construct an operational framework is, of course, the human dimension of the situation. The needs of the people involved in the leadership situation, both leaders and followers, vary according to any number of conditions. Sometimes strong leadership is welcomed, others rejected. There is, as Gardner notes, increasing support in the literature (Cleveland, 1993; Howard, 1998; Manz & Sims, 1993; Rost, 1991) for the view that the collaborative group is best served by a relationship in which the leader helps followers to develop their own judgment, enabling them to grow and become better contributors. Such an orientation helps to ensure that the institution can continue to thrive even after the leader's departure.

The question is how to best engender such a relationship. In the collaborative arrangement, how does one determine when to lead and when to follow? When should the line between leading and following be sharp and when should it be blurred? What sorts of strategies might a leader develop to "help followers develop their own judgment"? If the success of a collaborative effort lies in uniting the goals of its participants, how might those goals be discerned and assimilated? What if the goals are incompatible? What if they contradict the leader's professional judgment? Does our understanding of educational leadership even allow for the kind of collaborative relationship recommended by Rost wherein both leaders and followers "do" leadership? Or is that tantamount to the administrator's abdicating her/his leadership obligations?

STANDARD 5: INTEGRITY

Peter Block (1987) believes that principals have more potential to do good than they think:

> At the deepest level, the enemy of high performing systems is the feeling of helplessness that so many of us in organizations seem to experience. . . . The core of the bureaucratic mindset is not to take responsibility for what is happening. Other people are the problem. . . . Reawakening the original spirit means we have to confront the issue of our own autonomy. (pp. 1, 6)

Block argues further that leaders are too often preoccupied with "playing it safe," and thus adopt a maintenance strategy to leadership. To escape that strategy and to practice what he calls "enlightened self-interest," leaders have to first recognize their preoccupation, and then commit themselves to purposefully engaging in activities that have meaning (i.e., those which are genuinely necessary), that involve contribution and service, and that influence others' lives in a positive way. Whether we refer to those activities as moral or ethical, or as manifestations of values, beliefs, fairness, etc., all can be subsumed under the rubric of integrity.

One of the normative assumptions grounding the portfolio project, discussed in the introductory course, is that the development of the portfolio connects you to your own definition of leadership by giving you an opportunity to not only demonstrate some of the attributes which more conventional assessment instruments find immeasurable, but to do so in a way that enhances your internal consciousness of practice (i.e., your administrative literacy). Ezra Bowen defines a similar concept he refers to as "ethical literacy" (as cited in Ciulla, 1998), describing it as more than an ability to simply say yes or no to unambiguous alternatives. Ethical literacy "includes the discovering, anticipating, encountering, and constructing of moral problems, some of which are bona fide dilemmas, and the creating of workable solutions" (p. 372).

It is not, however, as Ciulla points out, what ethical literacy *is* but what it *does* that is important:

> [Ethical literacy] stimulates imagination and gives us a new way of seeing. Traditions can be assessed and reapplied and moral language can be woven into contexts and situations in ways that actually transform them. (p. 372)

Transforming tradition in a discipline that has often found it necessary to abandon idealism in the face of practical demands, however, may not be as easy as it sounds. Ciulla's discussion of business school students concerned about making it in the "real world" has a familiar ring:

> They want to live in [the real world] and don't want it to change in any fundamental way. It smacks of certainty and promise and appeals to those who pride themselves on having their feet planted squarely on the ground. Neither immoral nor amoral, the real world does not preclude morality—it just has a hard time making it fit in. (p. 373)

Many novice administrators make the same observation. They may have chosen to become principals because they thought they could have more of an impact on the lives of students by creating conditions that promote the likelihood of school improvement rather than by teaching children themselves. They may have entered the principal's office intending to focus on teaching and learning, on creating a more collegial atmosphere for teachers that is receptive to innovation or alternative evaluation. They may have had plans to influence the entire school culture by increasing shared decision-making and encouraging more collaborative planning with stakeholders.

What they say they find, discouragingly, is that all their good intentions to have a positive impact are subordinated to the demands of dealing with budgets, overseeing building management, meeting with outside influences (e.g., the board of education, parents, business leaders), handling policy mandates, negotiating staff conflicts, addressing student discipline, ensuring the school has adequate material resources and staff on hand, and in general responding to whatever crisis erupts at the moment.

The challenges of acting with integrity, however, are sometimes more formidable than recovering your sense of autonomy and finding the time to "fit in" an interest in morality. Even principals who wish to confront the Hobbesian assumption that self-interest is the primary motivation for human behavior can find the ambiguities that inhere in moral dilemmas debilitating to decision-making. What, for example, does one do when values are contested? Because life is necessarily value-laden, it is axiomatic that not all will share the same perspectives on what constitutes the right thing to do. How does a leader reconcile competing principles in order to establish a shared sense of values?

When the issue compels participants to consider the impact of their actions on others, how is it determined which others should take precedence? Such a dilemma is central to a number of currently contested initiatives in public education, among them the use of publicly funded vouchers for private school tuition and the establishment of an equitable funding system for public schools.

Sometimes the issues are less universal, but even more complicated. Perhaps the question isn't a matter of what's right for a class of people (e.g., faculty or students), but of what's right for an individual. How can a principal who perceives a course of action that's morally right for her/his school but compromises her/his own professional life make a decision? Judith Newman (1998) illustrates with this journal entry from a first-year teacher:

> After three years of waiting, I have finally signed a probationary contract. I'm bursting with excitement. On my first day at school, in the midst of my musings about how I can transform my classroom into an exciting place, a colleague drops by and introduces herself. We chat for a few minutes about her background and about the school community before she asks about some materials I've got laid out on a nearby table. I launch enthusiastically into an account of portfolio assessment. My colleague listens with the odd "uh-hum" and nod, and then she finally speaks. "We don't do stuff like that here. We'll hate you if you do because then we'll have to start doing the same thing." I chuckle nervously not knowing whether she is joking or being serious. Our chat ends soon after that. That was the first day. Four months later, I still have not implemented my portfolio plan.

Matters can become even more complex if the issue of economic welfare intrudes. While such situations are rare, how might a principal who discerns in a moral dilemma the possibility of job loss negotiate the competing moral exigencies? What if doing the right thing professionally endangers personal well-being?

You'll recall that we discussed the issue of choice as it relates to moral decision making (i.e., if there's truly no choice, a circumstance which is exceedingly rare, the issue isn't a moral one). It should be reiterated that many, if not most, circumstances which call for principals to act with integrity are not so unambiguous as to present only two alternatives, one "right" and one "wrong." What that means, of course, is that upholding your principles will sometimes require that other alternatives be identified; that when the present choices are unacceptable, others be generated. It is, however, human nature to attempt to reduce multifaceted moral problems into a dichotomous moral equation wherein the options are discrete. That renders decision making simple, and the tendency is magnified in institutions. How, then, does a principal attempt to create an environment in which "moral imagination" (Ciulla, 1998) flourishes? In which participants conceive of integrity not only as heightened moral awareness, but as finding creative ways to live up to those morals?

STANDARD 6: CONTEXT

Public education has always been at the center of our cultural evolution. This has been the case ever since Thomas Jefferson, remarking that every child, rich or poor, is capable of benefiting from an education and of being a better citizen by acquiring one, made the case for public schools. As we move into the next century, public education continues to be a primary participant in an environment of unprecedented social, political, and economic change. The speed and scope of technological advances, the emergence of a global economy, the rise of a multicultural workforce, the acceleration of geopolitical reconfigurations, and the reappearance of ethnic conflicts have steadily transformed our understandings of the world. Closer to home, some of the same forces have contributed to equally significant changes:

> It is estimated that 25 million Americans—20 percent of the workforce—were unemployed at some point in 1991. The United States has lost ground in key industrial sectors. . . . The federal debt tripled from $1.3 million to $3.6 trillion during the 1970s and 1980s. . . . The annual cost of servicing this debt is $360 billion. . . . The United States was once the world's largest creditor. It is now the world's largest debtor. Today's children will be the first generation in U.S. history to experience a lower standard of living than their parents. Infant mortality ranks with some third world countries despite much higher per capita health care costs compared with other Western economies. The infrastructure of roads, sewers,

> and the like is in serious decay. Homelessness is an international disgrace. Substantial numbers of people are socially and economically marginalized. . . . The dream of home ownership is becoming just a dream for millions of young people. Productivity of knowledge and service workers is a huge problem. (Tapscott & Caston, 1998, pp. 27–28)

The situation grew even more grim at the beginning of the new millennium. By mid-2003, the nation incurred the highest budget deficit in its history. Two consecutive tax cuts by the Bush administration had reduced revenues to the point that states, in desperate straits, started cutting funding to health care, education, and other social services. Highway maintenance was being postponed, other infrastructure projects cancelled altogether, and some states were even releasing prisoners from correctional facilities and delaying or deferring prosecutions to save money. By mid-2003, the unemployment rate had climbed to its highest level in nine years, and 56,000 jobs were lost in June alone. Phenomena such as these link people, institutions, and organizations in an environmental context of uncertainty where the only constant, as the maxim says, is change.

The dynamics of this environment require leadership that is not only aware of its shifting dimensions, but which can identify both the opportunities it represents and the problems it can produce. As appealing a prospect as it would be, public schools cannot remove themselves from the environmental context in which they exist. Both leaders and participants must determine what that context means to the school, and how the school can rise to the challenges it represents.

Why should public schools be concerned with issues other than their own immediate problems? Why, when faced with such matters as shrinking budgets, deteriorating facilities, insufficient numbers of faculty and staff, and inadequate materials, should principals consider the broader environment as well? The self-evident answer is that events in the wider public sphere necessarily influence those institutions supported by it. Public demands for more "accountability" in the form of higher standardized test scores, for example, can have a direct impact on school funding or closures, as can losses of revenue. The principal who chooses to be resolutely unaware of public attitudes and political and social circumstances risks putting her/his school at the mercy of them.

There is, however, a deeper reason for conceiving of the school not as an unwitting victim of prevailing environmental influences, but as a productive participant. By positioning themselves as an active part of the public sphere, public schools can achieve the purpose and legitimacy envisioned in the Jeffersonian mandate. By broadening our understanding of the "public" in public school, we create opportunities for putting our other principles to work.

We can share our microcosmic visions, showing how they exemplify the goals of a democratic society. We can bring our tradition of scholarship to the crafting of the public agenda as opposed to being a footnote therein, helping to produce the knowledge and understanding that leads to policy development. We can demonstrate our conceptions of stewardship and integrity in a collaborative effort to improve the conditions under which we all live and work. Perhaps most important, our students can gain a comprehensible "public" education, and even a sense of their collective power as citizens—what David Mathews (1999) calls "the power of relationships formed in doing public work" (p. 87).

The challenge for principals is to determine how to develop and prepare their faculties, staffs, and students for this understanding. How does one position the school for participation in the broader public sphere while still meeting its obligations to the school community? What skills will be necessary to prepare for that participation? How can the energies of faculty and staff, which are necessarily devoted to the school community, be marshaled for the commitment to a broader undertaking? How can students be engaged?

Warren Bennis and Burt Nanus (1998) point out that today's leaders are admired for their ability to "downsize, streamline and turn around organizations that have grown bloated and unwieldy." Tomorrow's leaders, however, "will be expected to create totally new organizational forms that position their enterprises in anticipation of future changes" (p. 6). While their remarks are intended for organizational leaders as opposed to school leaders, they have relevance. Tomorrow's principals, too, will have to conceive of new institutional forms that position their schools in anticipation of changes that will affect them. How can they best anticipate those changes and convert them into opportunities for their faculty and students?

APPENDIX G

Self- and Program Evaluation

The final step in completing the M.A. in leadership studies is the submission of the self- and program evaluations. Students will complete the evaluations subsequent to the successful presentation of the portfolio and submit them to the professor of record for LS 685. The questions are open-ended as the faculty believe such a format provides the greatest latitude to students in expressing themselves.

A. *Self-evaluation*. The purposes of the portfolio project are to give you the opportunity to discern, over time, aspects of administrative practice that have been established as the foundation of your own leadership philosophy, and to encourage your becoming a reflective practitioner. One of the ways to evaluate whether the process achieved those purposes is to employ the measure of consequential validity (i.e., whether its consequences have been positive). What have those consequences been for you? What impact did the construction of the portfolio have on you, in terms of both your professional and personal growth?

B. *Program evaluation*. Predicated on your self-evaluation, what comments/recommendations can you make concerning both the leadership studies program and the portfolio assessment itself? Did the construction of the portfolio (i.e., the documenting of your coursework, field experiences, reflections, and presentation of your work) give you ample opportunity to develop your leadership philosophy? To become a more reflective practitioner? To connect theory and practice? How might we strengthen the process?

APPENDIX H

Time Lines for Submission

Elements	*Entries*	*Time Frame*
Course Folios	Folio assignments for LS 500, 506, 510, 512, 515, 520, 530, 550, 600, 610, 630, and 675	@ completion of course
Field Experience Folio	Field experiences and subsequent reflections for LS 500, 506, 510, 512, 515, 520, 530, 550, 600, 610, 630, and 675	@ completion of field experience
Reflection Folio	Vision/ISLLC 1	@ completion of 6 hours of coursework
	Scholarship/ISLLC 2	@ completion of 12 hours of coursework
	Stewardship/ISLLC 3	@ completion of 18 hours of coursework
	Collaboration/ISLLC 4	@ completion of 24 hours of coursework
	Integrity/ISLLC 5	@ completion of 30 hours of coursework
	Context/ISLLC 6	@ completion of 36 hours of coursework
Portfolio	Preparation for symposium	During LS 685

APPENDIX I

Ethical Reasoning Model

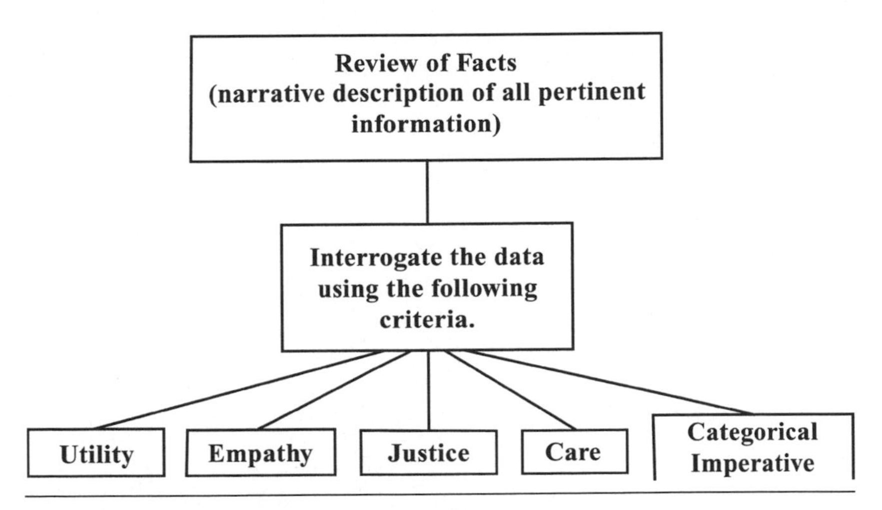

Source: Adapted from Holifield & Dickinson (2001, 47).

Bibliography

Adam, A. (1998). *Artificial knowing: Gender and the thinking machine*. New York: Routledge.

Alverno College Faculty. (1994). *Student assessment-as-learning at Alverno College*. Milwaukee: Alverno College Institute.

Anderson, M. (1989). Training and selecting school leaders. In S. Smith and P. Piele (Eds.), *School leadership: Handbook for excellence* (pp. 53–84). Eugene, OR: ERIC Clearinghouse on Educational Management, College of Education, University of Oregon.

Bailey, L. (1916). *The science spirit in a democracy: Ground levels in democracy*. Ithaca, NY: Privately published.

Barrett, B. (1995). Portfolio use in educational leadership programs: From theory to practice. *Innovative Higher Education, 19*(3), 197–206.

Barth, R. (1990). *Improving schools from within: Teachers, parents and principals can make the difference*. San Francisco: Jossey-Bass.

Bennis, W., & Nanus, B. (1998). Toward the new millennium. In G. Hickman (Ed.), *Leading organizations: Perspective for a new era* (pp. 5–7). Thousand Oaks, CA: Sage.

Blackman, M., & Fenwick, L. (2000). The principalship. *Education Week, 19*(29), 68, 46.

Bleakley, A. (1999). From reflective practice to holistic reflexivity. *Studies in Higher Education, 24*(3), 315–331.

Block, P. (1987). *The empowered manager: Positive political skills at work.* San Francisco: Jossey-Bass.

Bloom, A. (1987). *The closing of the American mind: How higher education has failed democracy and impoverished the souls of today's students*. New York: Simon & Schuster.

Bolin, F. (1988, March–April). Helping student teachers think about teaching. *Journal of Teacher Education, 39*(2), 48–54.

Bossert, S., Dwyer, D., Rowan, B., & Lee, G. (1982). The instructional management role of the principal. *Educational Administration Quarterly, 18*, 34–64.

Bredeson, P. (1995). Building a professional knowledge base in educational administration: Opportunities and obstacles. In R. Donmoyer, M. Imber, & J. Scheurich (Eds.), *The knowledge base in educational administration: Multiple perspectives* (pp. 47–61). Albany: State University of New York Press.

Brookover, W. (1981). *Effective secondary schools.* Philadelphia: Research for Better Schools.

Brown, G., & Irby, B. (1997). *The principal portfolio.* Thousand Oaks, CA: Corwin.

Brumbaugh, R. (1981). *The philosophers of Greece*. Albany: State University of New York Press.

Bruner, J. (1986). *Actual minds, possible worlds*. Cambridge, MA: Harvard University Press.

Bruner, J. (1994, April). *The human and interpretively possible*. Address at the annual meeting of the American Educational Research Association, New Orleans, LA.

Carlson, R. (1996). *Reframing and reform: Perspectives on organization, leadership and school change*. White Plains, NY: Longman.

Case, R. (1992). On the need to assess authentically. *Holistic Education Review, 5*(4), 14–23.

Chittenden, E., & Gardner, H. (1991). Authentic evaluation and documentation of student performance. In V. Perrone (Ed.), *Expanding student assessment* (pp. 22–31). Alexandria, VA: Association for Supervision and Curriculum Development.

Ciulla, J. (1998). Business ethics as moral imagination. In G. Hickman (Ed.), *Leading organizations: Perspectives for a new era* (pp. 372–377). Thousand Oaks, CA: Sage.

Clark, D., & Clark, S. (1996). Better preparation of educational leaders. *Educational Researcher, 25*(9), 18–20.

Clarke, A. (1995). Professional development in practicum settings: Reflective practice under scrutiny. *Teaching and Teacher Education, 11*(3), 243–261.

Cleveland, H. (1993, Summer). The twilight of hierarchy. *Kettering Review,* 48–52.

Cordeiro, P., & Smith-Sloan, E. (1995, April). *Apprenticeships for administrative interns: Learning to talk like a principal*. Paper presented at the annual meeting of the American Educational Research Association, San Francisco.

Crowson, R., & Porter-Gehrie, C. (1980). *The school principalship: An organizational stability role*. Paper presented at the annual meeting of the American Educational Research Association, Boston.

Cuban, L. (1988). *The managerial imperative and the practice of leadership in schools*. Albany: State University of New York Press.

Culbertson, J. (1988). A century's quest for a knowledge base. In N. Boyan (Ed.), *Handbook of research on educational administration* (pp. 3–26). New York: Longman.

Daresh, J. (1997, January). Improving principal preparation: A review of common strategies. *National Association of Secondary School Principals Bulletin*, 3–8.

Darling-Hammond, L. (1986). A proposal for evaluation in the teaching profession. *Elementary School Journal, 86*, 531–551.

Darling-Hammond, L. (1988). Accountability and teacher professionalism. *American Educator, 12*(4), 8–43.

Darling-Hammond, L. (1993, June). Reframing the school reform agenda. *Phi Delta Kappan, 74*(10), 752–762.

Darling-Hammond, L., Ancess, J., & Falk, B. (1995). *Authentic assessment in action: Studies of schools and students at work*. New York: Teachers College Press.

Dawson, C. (n.d.). *Peter Ramus* [Online]. Retrieved January 3, 2003, from http//www.lcc.gaatech.edu/gallery/rhetoric/figures/ramus.html.

DePree, M. (1989). *Leadership is an art*. New York: Doubleday.

Dess, G., & Miller, A. (1993). *Strategic management*. New York: McGraw-Hill.

Dewey, J. (1916). *Democracy and education*. New York: Macmillan.

Donmoyer, R. (1995). A knowledge base for educational administration: Notes from the field. In R. Donmoyer, M. Imber, & J. Scheurich (Eds.), *The knowledge base in educational administration: Multiple perspectives* (pp. 74–95). Albany: State University of New York Press.

Donmoyer, R., Imber, M., & Scheurich, J. (Eds.). (1995). *The knowledge base in educational administration: Multiple perspectives*. Albany: State University of New York Press.

Drucker, P. (1989). *The new realities*. New York: Harper & Row.

D'Souza, D. (1991). *Illiberal education: The politics of race and sex on campus*. New York: Free Press.

Duke, D. (1988). Why principals consider quitting. *Phi Delta Kappan, 70*(4), 308–313.

Ecclestone, K. (1996). The reflective practitioner: Mantra or model for emancipation? *Studies in the Education of Adults, 28,* 48–160.

Edmonds, R. (1979). Effective schools for the urban poor. *Educational Leadership, 39*, 15–27.

Edu-con. (1984). *The role of the public school principal in the Toronto Board of Education*. Toronto: Edu-con of Canada.

Ferrandino, V. (2001). Surviving a crisis. *Principal, 80*(4), 72.

Ferrandino, V., & Tirozzi, G. (2000). Our time has come. *NAESP Online* [Online]. Retrieved June 16, 2002, from http://www.naesp.org/misc/edweek_article_2-23-00.htm.

Frankl, V. (1959). *Man's search for meaning*. Boston: Beacon.

Freidus, H. (1996, April). *Reflection in teaching: Can it be taught?* Town meeting presentation at the annual meeting of the American Educational Research Association, New York.

Freidus, H. (1998). Mentoring portfolio development. In N. Lyons (Ed.), *With portfolio in hand: Validating the new teacher professionalism* (pp. 51–67). New York: Teachers College Press.

Fullan, M. (1988). *What's worth fighting for in the principalship*. Toronto: Ontario Public School Teachers' Federation.

Fullan, M. (1991). *The new meaning of educational change*. New York: Teachers College Press.

Gage, N. (1989). The paradigm wars and their aftermath: A "historical" sketch of research on teaching since 1989. *Educational Researcher, 18*(7), 4–10.

Gardner, J. (1987). Leaders and followers. *Liberal Education, 73*(2), 4–6.

Geltner, B. (1993, October). *Integrating formative portfolio assessment, reflective practice and cognitive coaching into preservice preparation*. Paper presented at the annual meeting of the University Council for Educational Administration, Houston.

Gilman, D., & Lanman-Givens, B. (2001). Where have all the principals gone? *Educational Leadership, 58*(8), 72–74.

Glaser, R. (1987). Thoughts on expertise. In C. Schooler and K.W. Schaie (Eds.), *Cognitive functioning and social structure over the life course* (pp. 81–94). Norwood, NJ: Ablex.

Green, J., & Smyser, S. (1996). *The teacher portfolio: A strategy for professional development and evaluation*. Lancaster, PA: Technomic.

Greene, M. (1994). Epistemology and educational research: The influence of recent approaches to knowledge. In L. Darling-Hammond (Ed.), *Review of research in education* (pp. 423–464). Washington, DC: American Educational Research Association.

Greenleaf, R. (1977). *Servant leadership: A journey into the nature of legitimate power and greatness*. New York: Paulist Press.

Greenleaf, R. (1998). Servant leadership in business. In G. Hickman (Ed.), *Leading organizations: Perspectives for a new era* (pp. 115–129). Thousand Oaks, CA: Sage.

Griffiths, D. (1988a). A century's quest for a knowledge base. In N. Boyan (Ed.), *Handbook of research on educational administration* (pp. 27–52). New York: Longman.

Griffiths, D. (1988b). *Educational administration: Reform PDQ or RIP* (University Council for Educational Administration, Occasional Paper No. 8312). Tempe: Arizona State University.

Guba, E., & Lincoln, Y. (1994). Competing paradigms in qualitative research. In N. Denton & Y. Lincoln (Eds.), *The handbook of qualitative research* (pp. 105–117). Thousand Oaks, CA: Sage.

Hackmann, D., & English, F. (2001, Spring). About straw horses and administrator shortages: Confronting the pragmatics of the administrative internship. *UCEA Review, 50*(2), 12–15.

Hackmann, D., Schmitt-Oliver, D., & Tracy, J. (2002). *The standards-based administrative internship: Putting the ISLLC standards into practice*. Lanham, MD: Scarecrow.

Hall, G. (1988). The principal as leader of the change facilitating team: Four studies using different disciplinary perspectives of the principal's role in change. *Journal of Research and Development in Education, 22*(1), 49–59.

Harding, T. (1940). Science and agricultural policy. In *Farmer in a changing world: Yearbook of agriculture*. Washington, DC: U.S. Department of Agriculture.

Harris, S. (1999). Re-live and learn: Hands-on research brings history home. *Virginia Tech Research* [Online]. Retrieved January 13, 2004, from http://www.research.vt.edu/resmag/1999resmag/index.html.

Hart, A., & Pounder, D. (1999). Reinventing preparation programs: A decade of activity. In J. Murphy & P. Forsyth (Eds.), *Educational administration: A decade of reform* (pp. 115–151). Thousand Oaks, CA: Corwin.

Herlong, A. (August, 1985). *Journalism in secondary education: Principles and guidelines for decision making within a systematic framework of moral alternatives*. Paper presented at the annual meeting of the Association for Education in Journalism and Mass Communication, Memphis.

Hickman, G. (Ed.). (1998). *Leading organizations: Perspectives for a new era*. Thousand Oaks, CA: Sage.

Hill, M., & Ragland, J. (1995). *Women as educational leaders: Opening windows, pushing ceilings*. Thousand Oaks, CA: Corwin.

Hirsch, E. (1987). *Cultural literacy: What every American needs to know*. Boston: Houghton Mifflin.

Holifield, M., & Dickinson, G. (2001). Ethical reasoning: A focus for program renewal. In F. Kochan & C. Reed (Eds.), *Education under construction: Southern Regional Council on Educational Administration*

2001 yearbook (pp. 41–47). Auburn, AL: Truman Pierce Institute, Auburn University.

Holmes Group. (1986). *Tomorrow's teachers: A report of the Holmes Group.* East Lansing, MI: Author.

House, E., & Lapan, S. (1978). *Survival in the classroom.* Boston: Allyn & Bacon.

Howard, A. (1998). The empowering leader: Unrealized opportunities. In G. Hickman (Ed.), *Leading organizations: Perspectives for a new era* (pp. 202–213). New York: Praeger.

Howe, K., & Eisenhart, M. (1990). Standards for qualitative (and quantitative) research: A prolegomenon. *Educational Researcher, 19*(4), 2–9.

Interstate School Leaders Licensure Consortium. (1996). *Standards for School Leaders.* Washington, DC: Council of Chief State School Officers.

Kempner, K. (1991). Getting into the castle of educational administration. *Peabody Journal of Education, 66*(3), 104–123.

LaBoskey, V. (1994). *Development of reflective practice.* New York: Teachers College Press.

LaBoskey, V. (1996, April). *Reflection in teaching: Can it be taught?* Town meeting presentation at the annual meeting of the American Educational Research Association, New York.

Lambert, L., Walker, D., Zimmerman, D., Cooper, J., Lambert, M., Gardner, M., et al. (1995). *The constructivist leader.* New York: Teachers College Press.

Lanham, R. (1993). *The electronic word: Democracy, technology and the arts.* Chicago: University of Chicago Press.

Lather, P. (1992). Critical frames in educational research: Feminist and post-structural perspectives. *Theory into Practice, 31*(2), 1–13.

Leary, P., & Nicholson, B. (2000, November). *The efficacy and appropriateness of a principal training program in Appalachia.* Paper presented at the annual meeting of the Southern Regional Council on Educational Administration, Nashville.

Leithwood, K. (1995). Preparing school leaders: What works? *Connections! 3*(3), 1–7.

Leithwood, K., & Jantzi, D. (1990, June). *Transformational leadership: How principals can help reform school culture.* Paper presented at the annual meeting of the Canadian Association for Curriculum Studies, Victoria, British Columbia.

Leithwood, K., & Montgomery, D. (1986). *The principal profile.* Toronto: OISE Press.

Leithwood, K., & Steinbach, R. (1995). *Expert problem solving: Evidence from school and district leaders.* Albany: State University of New York Press.

Lewis, A. (1996). Questions and answers about school leadership. *Phi Delta Kappan, 77*(8), 525–526.

Lezotte, L., Hathaway, D., Miller, S., Passalacqua, J., & Brookover, W. (1980). *School learning climate and student achievement*. East Lansing: Michigan State University, Center for Urban Affairs.

Lincoln, Y. (1994). Tracks toward a postmodern politics of evaluation. *Evaluation Practice, 15*(3), 299–309.

Lincoln, Y. (1995). Emerging criteria for quality in qualitative and interpretive research. *Qualitative Inquiry, 1*(3), 275–290.

Littrell, J., & Foster, W. (1995). The myth of a knowledge base in educational administration. In R. Donmoyer, M. Imber, & J. Scheurich (Eds.), *The knowledge base in educational administration: Multiple perspectives* (pp. 32–46). Albany: State University of New York Press.

Louis, K., & Miles, M. (1990). *Improving the urban high school: What works and why*. New York: Teachers College Press.

Louis, K., & Murphy, J. (1994). The evolving role of the principal. In J. Murphy and K. Louis (Eds.), *Reshaping the principalship: Insights from transformational reform efforts* (pp. 265–279). Thousand Oaks, CA: Corwin.

Lyons, N. (Ed.). (1998). *With portfolio in hand: Validating the new teacher professionalism*. New York: Teachers College Press.

Lyons, N., & Faculty of the University of Southern Maine's Extended Teacher Education Program. (1995). *Which standards? What performance? For what vision of teaching and learning?* Unpublished manuscript. University of Southern Maine, Gorham, ME.

Mabry, L. (1999). Writing to the rubric. *Phi Delta Kappan, 80*(9), 673–680.

MacIsaac, D. (1991). *Teacher induction partnerships: Portfolio development guide*. Greeley: University of Northern Colorado.

Manasse, L. (1985). Improving conditions for principal effectiveness. *Elementary School Journal, 85,* 439–463.

Manz, C., & Sims, H. (1993). *Business without bosses.* New York: Wiley.

Marsh, D. (1988, April). *Key factors associated with the effective implementation and impact of California's educational reform*. Paper presented at the annual meeting of the American Educational Research Association, New Orleans.

Martin, W., & Willower, D. (1981). The managerial behavior of high school principals. *Educational Administration Quarterly, 17*(1), 69–90.

Mathews, D. (1999). *Megachallenges: Higher Education Exchange*. Dayton, OH: Kettering Foundation.

McCloskey, D. (1985). *The rhetoric of economics*. Madison: University of Wisconsin Press.

Mertens, D. (1995). Identifying and respecting differences among participants in evaluation studies. In W. Shadish, D. Newman, M. Scheirer, & C. Wye (Eds.), *Guiding principles for evaluators. New Directions in Program Evaluation* (vol. 66, pp. 91–98). San Francisco: Jossey-Bass.

Mertens, D. (1998). *Research methods in education and psychology: Integrating diversity with quantitative and qualitative approaches.* Thousand Oaks, CA: Sage.

Miller, L. (1984). *American spirit: Visions of a new corporate culture*. New York: Morrow.

Morgan, P., Hertzog, C., & Gibbs, A. (2002). *Educational leadership: Performance standards, portfolio assessment, and the internship*. Lanham, MD: Scarecrow.

Mortimer, P., Sammons, P., Stoll, L., Lewis, D., & Ecob, R. (1988). *School matters: The junior years*. Sommerset, United Kingdom: Open Books.

Moss, P. (1997, March). *Developing coherence between assessment and reform in the licensing and professional development of teachers.* Paper presented at the annual meeting of the American Educational Research Association, Chicago.

Murphy, J. (1993). Alternative designs: New directions. In J. Murphy (Ed.), *Preparing tomorrow's school leaders: Alternative designs* (pp. 225–253). University Park, PA: University Council for Educational Administration.

Murphy, J. (1995a). The knowledge base in school administration: Historical footings and emerging trends. In R. Donmoyer, M. Imber, & J. Scheurich (Eds.), *The knowledge base in educational administration: Multiple perspectives* (pp. 62–73). Albany: State University of New York Press.

Murphy, J. (1995b). Rethinking the foundations of leadership preparation: Insights from school improvement efforts. *Design for leadership: The bulletin of the National Policy Board for Educational Administration, 6*(1), 1–4, 6.

Murphy, J., Shipman, N., & Thomson, S. (1996). *NCATE curriculum guidelines for educational leadership and the Interstate School Leaders Licensure Consortium standards.* Unpublished manuscript.

Muth, R. (1995). Craft knowledge and institutional constraints. In R. Donmoyer, M. Imber, & J. Scheurich (Eds.), *The knowledge base in educational administration: Multiple perspectives* (pp. 96–112). Albany: State University of New York Press.

Nanus, B. (1996). *Leading the way to organizational renewal*. Portland, OR: Productivity Press.

National Board for Professional Teaching Standards. (1989). *Toward high and rigorous standards for the teaching profession*. Washington, DC: Author.

National Council for Accreditation of Teacher Education. (1997). *NCATE 2000: Performance-based teacher education accreditation*. Washington, DC: Author.

National Policy Board for Educational Administration. (1989). *Improving the preparation of school administrators: An agenda for reform*. Charlottesville, VA: Author.

Newman, J. (1998, December). We can't get there from here: Critical issues in school reform. Retrieved June, 16, 2002, from http://www.pdkintl.org.

Nicholson, B., & Leary, P. (2001). Appalachian principals assess the efficacy and appropriateness of their training. *Planning and Changing, 32*(3–4), 199–213.

Nicolaides, N., & Gaynor, A. (1989). *The knowledge base informing the teaching of administrative and organizational theory in UCEA universities: Empirical and interpretive perspectives*. Charlottesville, VA: National Policy Board for Educational Administration.

Palmer, P. (1997, November–December). The heart of a teacher: Identity and integrity in teaching. *Change, 29*(6), 14–21.

Peters, S., Jordan, N., & Lemme, G. (1999). Toward a public science: Building a new social contract between science & society. *Higher Education Exchange*, 34–47.

Peterson, K. (1981, April). *Making sense of principal's work*. Paper presented at the annual meeting of the American Educational Research Association, Los Angeles.

Polanyi, M. (1996). *The tacit dimension*. New York: Doubleday.

Prestine, N. (1995). A constructivist view of the knowledge base in educational administration. In R. Donmoyer, M. Imber, & J. Scheurich (Eds.), *The knowledge base in educational administration: Multiple perspectives* (pp. 269–286). Albany: State University of New York Press.

Ross, D. (1990). Programmatic structures for the preparation of reflective teachers. In R. Clift, W. Houston, & M. Pugach (Eds.), *Encouraging reflective practice in education* (pp. 97–118). New York: Teachers College Press.

Rost, J. (1991). *Leadership for the 21st century.* New York: Praeger.

Ryan, K. (1998). Advantages and challenges of using inclusive evaluation approaches in evaluation practices. *American Journal of Evaluation, 98*(19), 101–123.

Sanford, J. (1995). Lessons of leadership: A critique of the knowledge base in educational administration. In R. Donmoyer, M. Imber, & J. Scheurich (Eds.), *The knowledge base in educational administration: Multiple perspectives* (pp. 182–194). Albany: State University of New York Press.

Sarason, S. (1982). *The culture of school and the problem of change*. Boston: Allyn & Bacon.

Sashkin, M. (1995). Visionary leadership. In J. Wren (Ed.), *The leader's companion: Insights on leadership through the ages* (pp. 402–407). New York: Free Press.

Schaefer, R. (1967). *The school as a center of inquiry*. New York: HarperCollins.

Scheurich, J. (1995). The knowledge base in educational administration: Postpositivist reflections. In R. Donmoyer, M. Imber, & J. Scheurich (Eds.), *The knowledge base in educational administration: Multiple perspectives* (pp. 17–31). Albany: State University of New York Press.

Schlechty, P. (1990). *Schools for the 21st century.* San Francisco: Jossey-Bass.

Schon, D. (1983). *The reflective practitioner*. New York: Basic Books.

Schon, D. (1987). *Educating the reflective practitioner: Toward a new design for teaching and learning in the professions*. San Francisco: Jossey-Bass.

Schulman, L. (1988). A union of insufficiencies: Strategies for teacher assessment in a period of educational reform. *Educational Leadership, 46*(3), 36–41.

Schulman, L. (1998). Teacher portfolios: A theoretical activity. In N. Lyons (Ed.), *With portfolio in hand: Validating the new teacher professionalism* (pp. 23–37). New York: Teachers College Press.

Schulman, L., Haertel, E., & Bird, T. (1988). *Toward alternative assessments of teaching: A report of a work in progress*. Stanford: Stanford University School of Education, Teacher Assessment Project.

Schwandt, T. (1989). Recapturing moral discourse in evaluation. *Educational Researcher, 18*(8), 11–16, 35.

Senge, P. (1990). *The fifth discipline: The art and practice of the learning organization*. New York: Doubleday.

Sergiovanni, T. (1990). *Value-added leadership: How to get extraordinary performance in schools*. San Diego: Harcourt Brace Jovanovich.

Sergiovanni, T. (1992). *Moral leadership: Getting to the heart of school improvement*. San Francisco: Jossey-Bass.

Sergiovanni, T. (1995). *The principalship: A reflective practice perspective*. Needham Heights, MA: Allyn & Bacon.

Sergiovanni, T. (1996). *Leadership for the schoolhouse: How is it different? Why is it important?* San Francisco: Jossey-Bass.

Shakeshaft, C. (1995). A cup half-full: A gender critique of the knowledge base in educational administration. In R. Donmoyer, M. Imber, & J. Scheurich (Eds.), *The knowledge base in educational administration: Multiple perspectives* (pp. 139–157). Albany: State University of New York Press.

Sirotnik, K. (1990). Society, schooling, teaching, and preparing to teach. In J. Goodlad, R. Soder, & K. Sirotnik (Eds.), *The moral dimensions of teaching* (pp. 296–327). San Francisco: Jossey-Bass.

Smith, J., & Heshusius, L. (1986, January). Closing down the conversation: The end of the quantitative-qualitative debate among educational inquirers. *Educational Researcher 5*(1), 4–12.

Smith, W., & Andrews, R. (1989). *Instructional leadership: How principals make a difference*. Alexandria, VA: Association for Supervision and Curriculum Development.

Snyder, J., Lippincott, A., & Bower, D. (1998). Portfolios in teacher education: Technical or transformational? In N. Lyons (Ed.), *With portfolio in hand: Validating the new teacher professionalism* (pp. 123–142). New York: Teachers College Press.

Sparkes, A. (1989). Paradigmatic confusions of the evasion of critical issues in naturalistic research. *Journal of Teaching in Physical Education, 8*, 131–151.

Sparks-Langer, G., & Colton, A. (1991, March). Synthesis of research on teachers' reflective thinking. *Educational Leadership, 48*, 37–44.

Stanfield, J., & Dennis, J. (Eds.) (1993). *Race and ethnicity in research methods.* Newbury Park, CA: Sage.

Tapscott, D., & Caston, A. (1998). Paradigm shift. In G. Hickman (Ed.), *Leading organizations: Perspectives for a new era* (pp. 26–43). Thousand Oaks, CA: Sage.

Teddlie, C., Kirby, P., & Stringfield, S. (1989). Effective versus ineffective schools: Observable differences in the classroom. *American Journal of Education, 97*, 221–236.

Thomson, S. (Ed.). (1993). *Principals for our changing schools: Knowledge and skill base*. Lancaster, PA: Technomic.

Thoreau, H. (1854). *Walden.* Retrieved October 10, 2002, from http://libws66.lib.niu.edu/thoreau/.

Thorndike, E. (1921). Measurement in education. *Teachers College Record, 22*, 378.

Thurston, P., Clift, R., & Schacht, M. (1993). Preparing leaders for change-oriented schools. *Phi Delta Kappan, 75*(3), 259–265.

Tierney, D. (1992). *Teaching portfolios: 1992 update on research and practice*. Los Angeles: Far West Laboratory for Educational Research and Development.

University Council for Educational Administration. (1992). *Essential knowledge for school leaders*. Unpublished proposal.

Usher, R., & Edwards, R. (1994). *Postmodernism and education*. London: Routledge.

Van Manen, M. (1977). Linking ways of knowing with ways of being practical. *Curriculum Inquiry, 6*(3), 205–228.

Vroom, V. (1964). *Work and motivation*. New York: Wiley.

Vygotsky, L. (1978). *Mind in society: The development of higher psychological processes.* (M. Cole, V. John-Steiner, S. Scribner, & E. Souberman, Eds.). Cambridge, MA: Harvard University Press.

Wheatley, M. (1994). *Leadership and the new science: Learning about organization from an orderly universe*. San Francisco: Berrett-Koehler.

Wilmore, E., & Erlandson, D. (1995, January). *Portfolio assessment in preparation of school administrators*. Paper presented at the annual meeting of the Southwest Educational Research Association, Dallas.

Wolcott, H. (1973). *The man in the principal's office*. New York: Holt, Rinehart & Winston.

Wolf, D. (1998). Creating a portfolio culture. In N. Lyons (Ed.), *With portfolio in hand: Validating the new teacher professionalism* (pp. 41–50). New York: Teachers College Press.

Yerkes, D. (1995). Developing a professional portfolio. *Thrust for Educational Leadership, 24*(5), 10–14.

Index

About the Author

Barbara L. Nicholson earned her Ph.D. from Ohio University in 1987 and is presently a professor of leadership studies in the Graduate School of Education and Professional Development at Marshall University. Her interest in assessment issues dates back to her employment in the administration of former West Virginia governor Gaston Caperton, who now chairs The College Board. Dr. Nicholson is a former Fulbright fellow to Uppsala University in Sweden, and has been a visiting professor in the Czech Republic, Northern Ireland, Russia, and Scotland. She is the author of numerous articles and presentations, both national and international, on issues related to alternative assessment and design of programs in preservice educational administration.